The Battle of Midway

Books in the Battle Series:

★ ★ ★ **Battles of World War II** ★ ★ ★

The Battle of Midway

by Earle Rice Jr.

Lucent Books, P.O. Box 289011, San Diego, CA 92198-9011

Library of Congress Cataloging-in-Publication Data

Rice, Earle, Jr.
    The Battle of Midway / by Earle Rice, Jr.
        p.   cm. — (Battles of World War II)
    Includes bibliographical references and index.
    ISBN 1-56006-415-3 (lib. ed. : alk. paper)
    1. Midway, Battle of, 1942—Juvenile literature. [1. Midway,
Battle of, 1942. 2. World War, 1939-1945—Pacific Ocean.]
I. Title. II. Series.
D774.M5R53
940.54'26—dc20   95-12206
                                                                        CIP
                                                                        AC

Contents

Foreword

Almost everyone would agree with William Tecumseh Sherman that war "is all hell." Yet the history of war, and battles in particular, is so fraught with the full spectrum of human emotion and action that it becomes a microcosm of the human experience. Soldiers' lives are condensed and crystallized in a single battle. As Francis Miller explains in his *Photographic History of the Civil War* when describing the war wounded, "It is sudden, the transition from marching bravely at morning on two sound legs, grasping your rifle in two sturdy arms, to lying at nightfall under a tree with a member forever gone."

Decisions made on the battlefield can mean the lives of thousands. A general's pique or indigestion can result in the difference between life and death. Some historians speculate, for example, that Napoleon's fateful defeat at Waterloo was due to the beginnings of stomach cancer. His stomach pain may have been the reason that the normally decisive general was sluggish and reluctant to move his troops. And what kept George McClellan from winning battles during the Civil War? Some scholars and contemporaries believe that it was simple cowardice and fear. Others argue that he felt a gut-wrenching unwillingness to engage in the war of attrition that was characteristic of that particular conflict.

Battle decisions can be magnificently brilliant and horribly costly. At the Battle of Thaspus in 47 B.C., for example, Julius Caesar, facing a numerically superior army, shrewdly ordered his troops onto a narrow strip of land bordering the sea. Just as he expected, his enemy thought he had accidentally trapped himself and divided their forces to surround his troops. By dividing their army, his enemy had given Caesar the strategic edge he needed to defeat them. Other battle orders result in disaster, as in the case of the Battle at Balaklava during the Crimean War in 1854. A British general gave the order to attack a force of withdrawing enemy Russians. But confusion in relaying the order resulted in the 670 men of the Light Brigade's charging in the wrong direction into certain death by heavy enemy cannon fire. Battles are the stuff of history on the grandest scale—their outcomes often determine whether nations are enslaved or liberated.

Moments in battles illustrate the best and worst of human character. In the feeling of terror and the us-versus-them attitude that accompanies war, the enemy can be dehumanized and treated with a contempt that is considered repellent in times of peace. At Wounded Knee, the distrust and anticipation of violence that grew between the Native Americans and American soldiers led to the senseless killing of ninety men, women, and children. And who can forget My Lai, where the deaths of old men, women, and children at the hands of American soldiers shocked an America already disillusioned with the Vietnam War. The murder of six million Jews will remain burned into the human conscience forever as the measure of man's inhumanity to man. These horrors cannot be forgotten. And yet, under the terrible conditions of battle, one can find acts of bravery, kindness, and altruism. During the Battle of Midway, the members of Torpedo Squadron 8, flying in hopelessly antiquated planes and without the benefit of air protection from fighters, tried bravely to fulfill their mission—to destroy the *Kido Butai,* the Japanese Carrier Striking Force. Without air support, the squadron was immediately set upon by Japanese fighters. Nevertheless, each bomber tried valiantly to hit his target. Each failed. Every man but one died in the effort. But by keeping the Japanese fighters busy, the squadron bought time and delayed further Japanese fighter attacks. In the aftermath of the Battle of Isandhlwana in South Africa in 1879, a force of thousands of Zulu warriors trapped a contingent of British troops in a small trading post. After repeated bloody attacks in which many died on both sides, the Zulus, their final victory certain, granted the remaining British their lives as a gesture of respect for their bravery. During World War I, American troops were so touched by the fate of French war orphans that they took up a collection to help them. During the Civil War, soldiers of the North and South would briefly forget that they were enemies and share smokes and coffee across battle lines during the endless nights. These acts seem all the more dramatic, more uplifting, because they indicate that people can continue to behave with humanity when faced with inhumanity.

Lucent Books' Battles Series highlights the vast range of the human character revealed in the ordeal of war. Dramatic narrative describes in exciting and accurate detail the commanders, soldiers, weapons, strategies, and maneuvers involved in each battle. Each volume includes a comprehensive historical context, explaining what brought the parties to war, the events leading to the battle, what factors made the battle important, and the effects it had on the larger war and later events.

The Battles Series also includes a chronology of important dates that gives students an overview, at a glance, of each battle. Sidebars create a broader context by adding enlightening details on leaders, institutions, customs, warships, weapons, and armor mentioned in the narration. Every volume contains numerous maps that allow readers to better visualize troop movements and strategies. In addition, numerous primary and secondary source quotations drawn from both past historical witnesses and modern historians are included. These quotations demonstrate to readers how and where historians derive information about past events. Finally, the volumes in the Battles Series provide a launching point for further reading and research. Each book contains a bibliography designed for student research, as well as a second bibliography that includes the works the author consulted while compiling the book.

Above all, the Battles Series helps illustrate the words of Herodotus, the fifth-century B.C. Greek historian now known as the "father of history." In the opening lines of his great chronicle of the Greek and Persian Wars, the world's first battle book, he set for himself this goal: "To preserve the memory of the past by putting on record the astonishing achievements both of our own and of other peoples; and more particularly, to show how they came into conflict."

Chronology of Events

1931
September Japanese army occupies south and central Manchuria.

1937
July 7 Japanese troops clash with Chinese troops near Peiping (now Beijing) marking the beginning of Sino-Japanese War.

1940
September 27 Japan signs Tripartite Pact to become ally of Hitler's Germany and Mussolini's Italy.

1941
December 7 Japanese carrier force led by Vice Admiral Chuichi Nagumo attacks U.S. naval base at Pearl Harbor.

1942
April 18 Colonel James H. Doolittle leads bombing raid on Tokyo.

May 6 Americans surrender Corregidor to Japanese army.

May 7–8 Battle of the Coral Sea.

May 26–29 Admiral Isoroku Yamamoto's Combined Fleet leaves bases in Japan bound for Midway and the Aleutians.

May 28 Task Force 16 departs Pearl Harbor for Point Luck.

May 30 Task Force 17 departs Pearl Harbor for Point Luck.

June 2 Task Forces 16 and 17 meet at Point Luck.

June 3

0900 Ensign Jewell "Jack" Reid reports "Sighted main body."

1640 B-17s attack Japanese Transport Group; no hits.

1950 Rear Admiral Frank Jack Fletcher corrects course to the southwest.

June 4

0430 Admiral Nagumo begins to launch Midway attack wave.

0500 Japanese heavy cruiser *Tone* launches Number Four observation plane.

0530 Lieutenants Howard Ady and William Chase report "Enemy carriers."

0630 Nagumo's attack wave strikes Midway Atoll.

0700 Tomonaga radios "There is need for a second attack."

0706 *Enterprise* and *Hornet* commence launching.

0708 Midway-based Marauders and Avengers attack *Akagi*.

0715 Nagumo orders planes to reequip with bombs for second attack on Midway.

0728 *Tone* Number Four plane reports "10 ships, probably enemy."

0745 Nagumo decides to interrupt rearming of planes from torpedoes to bombs.

0748 VMSB-241 aircraft attack *Kido Butai*.

0807 Nagumo decides to continue rearming of planes from torpedoes to bombs.

0810 B-17s bomb carriers; no hits.

0820 *Tone* Number Four plane reports sighting enemy aircraft carrier.

0822 Nagumo orders rearming of planes from bombs to torpedoes.

0837 *Akagi* starts landing Tomonaga's planes (back from Midway).

0918 Nagumo shifts course 90° and steams to meet American fleet.

0920 Torpedo (squadron) 8 attacks *Kido Butai*.

0940 Torpedo (squadrons) 3 and 6 attack *Kido Butai.*

0948 Lieutenant Commander Clarence W. McClusky Jr. decides to start flying northwest.

0955 McClusky sights destroyer's wake and follows.

1024–1030 "Six minutes that changed the world": American dive-bombers (VB-3, VB-6, and VS-6) attack *Kido Butai.*

1040 *Hiryu* launches first attack wave against *Yorktown.*

1200 *Hiryu* aircraft commence first attack on *Yorktown.*

1245 *Hiryu* launches second attack wave against *Yorktown.*

1434 *Hiryu* aircraft commence second attack on *Yorktown.*

1455 Captain Elliot Buckmaster orders *Yorktown* abandoned.

1550 *Enterprise* launches dive-bomber attack wave (VB-3, VB-6, and VS-6) against *Hiryu.*

1645 Lieutenant W. Earl Gallaher sights *Hiryu.*

1700 Dive-bombers from *Enterprise* attack *Hiryu.*

1712 VB-8 and VS-8 bombers attack *Tone* and *Chikuma*; no hits.

1745 B-17s from Midway and Molokai attack *Tone* and *Chikuma*; no hits.

1915 *Soryu* sinks; VMSB-241 planes depart Midway for night attack but return without sighting *Kido Butai.*

1925 *Kaga* sinks.

2340 Nagumo ordered to turn around and participate in night engagement.

June 5

0255 Admiral Yamamoto cancels Midway operation.

0355 U.S. submarine *Tambor* tracks Japanese cruiser force.

0500 *Akagi* scuttled.

0745 VMSB-241 bombers attack *Mikuma* and *Mogami.*

0900 *Hiryu* sinks.

1200 *Vireo* takes *Yorktown* in tow.

June 6

0510 *Enterprise* sends out eighteen scout planes.

0645 *Enterprise* scout reports sighting a carrier and five destroyers (false); a second scout reports sighting two heavy cruisers and three destroyers at 0730.

0757 *Hornet* launches twenty-six dive-bombers and eight fighters.

0950 *Hornet* planes attack cruiser group; score hits on *Mikuma*, *Mogami*, and *Asashio,* inflicting minor damage.

1045 *Enterprise* launches thirty-one dive-bombers, twelve fighters, and three torpedo bombers.

1230 *Enterprise* planes attack cruiser group; *Mikuma* and *Mogami* hit; severe damage to both.

1330 *Hornet* launches second attack against cruiser group.

1445 *Hornet* planes attack cruiser group again, hitting *Mikuma* and destroyer *Asashio.*

June 7

0458 *Yorktown* sinks.

INTRODUCTION

Shadows from a Rising Sun

The Battle of Midway was perhaps the greatest sea battle ever fought. The battle began on June 4 and ended on June 6, 1942, one day shy of six months after the Japanese sneak attack on Pearl Harbor. It ended in what historian Walter Lord called an "incredible victory" over a massive Japanese naval force by a much smaller American fleet. The American victory at Midway marked a turning point in the Pacific, stripping Japan of the initiative, and forcing the Japanese navy on the defensive for the first time in the war. Japan never regained the offensive.

Amazingly, the American navy seized victory from the near-certainty of defeat in the space of one-tenth of an hour. The famous American naval historian and former rear admiral Samuel Eliot Morison described that brief moment of strife as "six minutes that changed the world." A perfect union of luck, guts, indomitable will, and enemy errors in judgment enabled an American triumph in the face of overwhelming opposition. The odds against such a union at just the right time (from an American perspective) would seem to exceed the merely incredible. Perhaps what happened in those six momentous minutes really was—in the splendid phrasing of Gordon W. Prange—a "miracle at Midway."

Code of the *Kodo-Ha*

During the 1920s, a political movement not unlike Hitler's National Socialism took root in Japan and began to grow steadily stronger. Known as *Kodo-Ha* (the Way of the Emperor), the movement supported a totalitarian state controlled by the army.

Internally, *Kodo-Ha* extremists hoped to abolish the power of major capitalists and rid Japan of liberalism and Western influences. Externally, they supported a policy of total Japanese supremacy in the Far East. They envisioned as an end goal "the eight corners of the world under one roof," with Japan ascending to a dominant position in the world.

Asia for Asians

In 1931 the Japanese army embarked on a policy of expansion inspired by the powerful Kodo element within its ranks. It first overran Manchuria, eventually converting it into a puppet state, renamed Manchukuo. The League of Nations—a group of some sixty nations formed after World War I with the aim of preventing war—quickly condemned Japan for its aggression. Japan responded by resigning its membership.

A minor scuffle between Japanese and Chinese troops near Peiping (now Beijing) on July 7, 1937, escalated into the Sino-Japanese War. Japan invaded China and occupied much of China's coastal area, including many important cities and seaports. Japan tried to downplay its aggression in the eyes of the world by referring to the conflict as the China Incident. In reality the "incident" was a full-scale, bloody war.

Evolving rapidly now among the more militant members of Japan's government was the concept of the "Greater East Asia Co-Prosperity Sphere." Originated by General Hachiro Arita while he served as Japan's minister of foreign affairs, it called for recognition of economic and political ties between the Japanese Empire and the "Southern Regions." The Southern Regions included the East Indies, Malaya, the Philippines, Java, Sumatra, Burma (now

Japanese troops occupy Shanghai during the Sino-Japanese War in 1937.

Military Twenty-Four-Hour Clock

Military times are used throughout the book. This key, showing familiar A.M. and P.M. times paired with the corresponding time on the twenty-four-hour clock, may be helpful in learning the system.

A.M.	24	P.M.	24
1	0100	1	1300
2	0200	2	1400
3	0300	3	1500
4	0400	4	1600
5	0500	5	1700
6	0600	6	1800
7	0700	7	1900
8	0800	8	2000
9	0900	9	2100
10	1000	10	2200
11	1100	11	2300
12	1200	12	2400

Myanmar), and Thailand—all nations rich in raw materials. Arita's concept supposedly represented an appeal for Asian unity (with the apparent exclusion of China). But in truth the real and ultimate aim of his "Asia for Asians" plea was the acquisition of oil to fuel Japan's war machine. And Sumatra and the East Indies (now Indonesia), of course, owned rich oil resources.

Japan Joins the Axis

Japanese expansion continued in the spring of 1939, with the occupation of the strategic island of Hainan in the South China Sea. After the fall of France in May 1940, Japanese troops moved into northern Indochina (now Vietnam), which was then a French colony. The government of France, temporarily based in Vichy, in the central part of the country, was then under Nazi control and powerless to prevent the Japanese intrusion. Accordingly, France granted Japan rights of passage in Indochina. Japan, in return for these "transit" privileges, supposedly recognized France's right of rule in Indochina. By midsummer of the following year, Japanese forces occupied all of Indochina. Each move brought Japan closer to the Southern Regions.

On September 27, 1940, Japan signed an agreement known as the Tripartite Pact and entered into a military alliance with Germany and Italy. Together, the three countries became known as the Axis powers, or simply the Axis. As a member of this Rome-Berlin-Tokyo axis, Japan recognized the "New Order in

Japanese troops advance into Indochina from southwest China. In 1940, Japan entered into the Tripartite Pact with Adolf Hitler (right) and Benito Mussolini (left).

Three-Power Pact

To better acquaint his military commanders and high-ranking diplomats with the aims of his new agreement with Japan, the German dictator Adolf Hitler issued a top-secret directive on March 5, 1941. The directive, entitled "Basic Order No. 24 Regarding Collaboration [working together] with Japan," included this summary (the italics are Hitler's).

> It must be the *aim* of the collaboration based on the Three-Power Pact to induce Japan as soon as possible to *take active measures in the Far East*. Strong British forces will thereby be tied down, and the center of gravity of the interests of the United States will be diverted to the Pacific. . . .
>
> The *common aim* of the conduct of the war is to be stressed as forcing England to her knees quickly and thereby keeping the United States out of the war.

The *seizure of Singapore* as the key British position in the Far East would mean a decisive success for the entire conduct of war of the Three Powers.

The charismatic Hitler masterminded Germany's World War II effort.

Europe," championed by Adolf Hitler, the leader of Nazi Germany, and embraced by Benito Mussolini, the Fascist premier of Italy. Germany and Italy in return acknowledged "the leadership of Japan in the establishment of a New Order in Greater East Asia." Each country pledged to aid the other if "attacked by a power not presently involved in the European war or in the Sino-Japanese conflict." Insofar as Japan was concerned, such a "power" could only mean the United States, Japan's only rival for naval supremacy in the Pacific Ocean.

Rumors of War

Exactly four months later, on January 27, 1941, Joseph C. Grew, the U.S. ambassador to Japan, noted in his diary: "There is a lot of talk around town to the effect that the Japanese, in case of a break with the United States, are planning to go all out in a surprise mass attack at Pearl Harbor. Of course I informed our government."

Before the Japanese attack on Pearl Harbor, most people in the United States had refused to believe that Japan posed a threat to the comfortable American way of life. They chose to ignore ample warnings that such an attack might come at any time. The view that those Americans must, to some degree, share the blame for its happening was expressed in a cutting newspaper editorial:

"In a sense we were all out there," the Milwaukee *Journal* declared on January 27, 1942.

"We were all substituting our 'beliefs' for factual information available. The Axis had shown that it was out to conquer the world. A good many people did not want to believe that, so they didn't. Axis powers had demonstrated that they would strike friend or foe without warning. That was not a comfortable thought, so discard it. The time was short—too short—but if we adopted that idea we should have to pursue a course which would interfere with 'life as usual.' So we pushed aside the disagreeable warnings. . . .

"We thought we could pursue our peaceful, often lax, always controversial way and be safe from a nation that had determined to challenge us in the Pacific, and prepared for 10 years to do this, and had behind it years of military training."

Grew had no way of knowing at the time that Admiral Isoroku Yamamoto, commander in chief of the Combined Japanese Fleet, was already planning the Pearl Harbor attack.

Yamamoto, the revered "father of Japanese aviation," was a product of the Imperial Naval Academy, thought to own the sharpest mind in the Japanese navy. He had served in the Japanese embassy in Washington, D.C., during 1925–27 after doing postgraduate work at Harvard. He both liked and respected Americans, and, like most leaders of the Imperial Navy, opposed entering a war with the United States. Yamamoto had also opposed the pact with the Axis. He both distrusted the Germans and respected the enormous industrial potential of the United States. A union with Berlin and Rome, he feared, would inevitably move Japan closer to war with the Americans. And war with the Americans might prove disastrous to his beloved country.

Because of his opposing views, Yamamoto had risked becoming a target for political assassination by fanatical "Greater East Asia" supporters. Prominent among those fanatics was General Hideki Tojo, leader of the Kodo "war" party (and soon to become Japan's minister of foreign affairs). Yamamoto could voice his dissent, but he could not stifle the winds of change that were blowing hard across his land. But if war became unavoidable, Yamamoto, true patriot that he was, would be ready.

Day of Infamy

On July 25, 1941, Japan completed arrangements with the Vichy government to occupy central and southern Indochina as well as the northern portion, which Japan had invaded in 1940. Again powerless to object, the Vichy government granted Japan permission to occupy the rest of Indochina. Japan willingly accepted under the weak excuse of "protecting" Indochina.

President Franklin D. Roosevelt countered Japan's continued expansion by issuing an executive order the next day, freezing Japanese assets in the United States. His order effectively choked off all Japanese-American trade and cut off vital U.S. oil exports.

Japan had managed to store enough oil for about one year of war. Even normal peacetime needs would put a strain on the nation's oil reserves shortly thereafter. Since Japan imported about 80 percent of its oil from the United States, the trade stoppage meant only two choices to the expansionist Japanese: Japan could either seek a reversal of Roosevelt's new policy, or it could go to war with the United States. Either way, Japan faced the need for a quick decision. The world learned of that decision on December 7, 1941, which President Roosevelt immediately marked as "a date that will live in infamy."

At 0755 on that calm Sunday morning, 353 aircraft of Japanese vice admiral Chuichi Nagumo's First Air Fleet commenced an assault on the U.S. Pacific Fleet moored at Pearl Harbor and the

military airfields on the Hawaiian island of Oahu. The Japanese attackers achieved complete surprise. Nagumo's raiders accomplished their mission in less than two hours and disappeared over the northwest horizon, leaving behind death and destruction.

In addition to 2,403 Americans killed and 1,178 wounded, 18 U.S. ships had been sunk or badly damaged. Of a total of 394 U.S. planes, 188 were destroyed and 159 damaged. Property damage totaled well into the millions of dollars. Damage to the Navy Yard alone was estimated at $42 million. Congress called the attack on Pearl Harbor "the greatest military and naval disaster in our nation's history."

The one bright spot in America's darkest day was that the carriers *Enterprise*, *Lexington*, and *Saratoga* were not in port at the time of the attack. Their loss would have severely impacted the U.S. Navy's ability to strike back at Japan, possibly adding years to the war's duration.

The Japanese lost twenty-nine airplanes belonging to the First Air Fleet, five midget submarines, and one full-size submarine. The submarines formed a part of "Special Naval Attack Unit" that had deployed at Pearl Harbor in advance of the main strike force and subsequently played a minor role in the attack.

Isoroku Yamamoto, commander in chief of the Combined Japanese Fleet, was the military genius behind the Japanese attack on Pearl Harbor (top). (Middle) The USS Arizona *is hit by Japanese air fire during the attack on Pearl Harbor. Franklin Roosevelt signs a war declaration against Japan in response to the attack (bottom).*

Pearl Harbor Only a "Supporting Operation"

According to Mitsuo Fuchida and Masatake Okumiya, naval officers who took part in the Battle of Midway, "the primary objective of our [the Japanese] war strategy was to secure oil resources. The Pearl Harbor attack itself [which had been led by Fuchida] was conceived purely as a supporting operation toward that objective. As our military resources were limited and oil was our immediate goal, there was no reason to contemplate the seizure of the Hawaiian territory." After the attack, however, the Japanese realized that greater harm could and should have been inflicted upon the enemy.

"All in all," Fuchida and Okumiya continued, "the Pearl Harbor operation did achieve its basic strategic objective of preventing the U.S. Pacific Fleet from interfering with Japanese operations in the south. But the failure to inflict any damage on the enemy carriers still weighed heavily on the minds of Admiral Nagumo's air staff and flying officers as the task force cruised back toward home waters. We immediately began laying plans for subsequent operations to achieve what we had been unable to accomplish at Pearl Harbor."

War Plans

Japan accepted the losses as a small price to pay for having successfully carried out the primary intent of Operation Order Number 1, issued by Admiral Yamamoto on November 5, 1941. The order outlined the aims of what he termed the Hawaii Operation.

In part, the order stated: "In the East the American fleet will be destroyed. The American lines of operation and supply lines to the Orient will be cut. Enemy forces will be intercepted and annihilated. Victories will be exploited to break the enemy's will to fight." These key sentences summarize Japan's intended military strategy for the entire war.

The Unstoppable Japanese War Machine

On December 8 (December 7 to the east of the international date line), Japanese forces launched simultaneous attacks on Wake Island, Hong Kong, Malaya, Thailand, and the Philippines.

Two days later, a Japanese landing on Guam quickly overran a handful of sailors and marines.

Marines and sailors on Wake Island fought valiantly to repel the first Japanese landing on December 11, the only time during the war that an amphibious landing was repulsed. But the tiny garrison succumbed to a second enemy assault on December 23.

The U.S. Navy Yard is aflame during the Japanese attack on the Philippines. In the right center of the photo, a barge loaded with torpedoes is ablaze. The submarine at right was also damaged in the bombing.

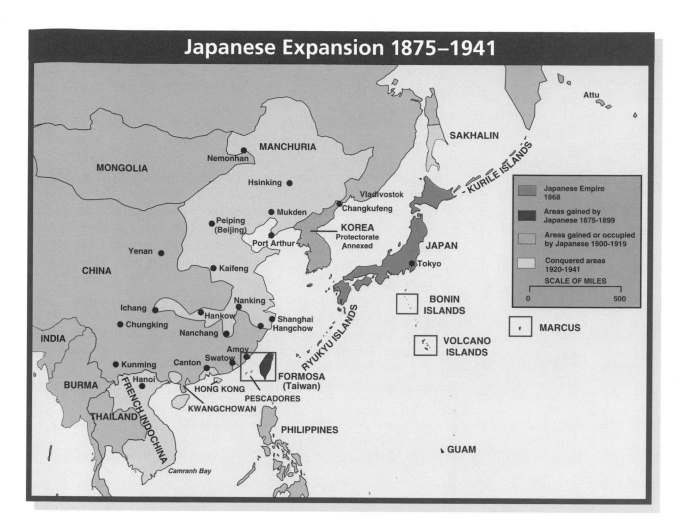

Japanese Expansion 1875–1941

Legend:
- Japanese Empire 1868
- Areas gained by Japanese 1875-1899
- Areas gained or occupied by Japanese 1900-1919
- Conquered areas 1920-1941

SCALE OF MILES
0   500

A final message sent from Wake Island to Pearl Harbor said: "ENEMY ON ISLAND . . . ISSUE IN DOUBT."

Stubborn British and Canadian defenders on the Crown Colony of Hong Kong held out an additional two days before they too surrendered to Japanese invaders on Christmas Day.

Following several small attacks on northern Luzon airfields, 142 Japanese planes struck hard at the Clark Field–Iba airdrome complex near Manila at 1215 on December 8. Most of America's Far Eastern air power was destroyed on the ground. Two days later, while Japanese bombers wrecked the U.S. naval base at Cavite, destroying ships and installations, Japanese ground forces began landing on Luzon. American and Filipino troops fought hard and well against a far larger Japanese army, withdrawing first to the Bataan Peninsula, and then to the fortified island of Corregidor in Manila Bay. Corregidor fell to the Japanese on May 6, 1942.

The Japanese wave swept south on December 8, mounting amphibious operations at Singora and Patani in southern Thailand and at Kota Bharu in northern Malaya.

In hopes of sinking the Japanese invasion vessels, the British battleship *Prince of Wales* and the battle cruiser *Repulse* dashed northward from Singapore. Unable to find the Japanese fleet, they set a return course for Singapore. Suddenly, they found themselves caught in a furious surface-air battle. In less than an hour, the two British warships were resting on the floor of the South China Sea. Only the three American carriers remained as serviceable Allied capital ships in the entire Pacific theater.

Japanese troops occupied Thailand quietly, then moved in steamroller fashion down both sides of the Malay Peninsula. By the end of January, the invaders had forced the outmaneuvered and outgunned British troops into a rapid withdrawal and a last-ditch battle for the supposedly impregnable island "fortress" of Singapore. Singapore's defenders surrendered unconditionally to the Japanese on February 15, 1942.

Immediately following the occupation of Thailand, the Japanese moved into Burma, launching attacks on Moulmein and Tavoy. The Japanese pressed steadily through Burma, forcing the opposing British and Chinese troops to retreat northward and

Both of the British warships Repulse *and* Prince of Wales *were sunk by the Japanese in a battle that lasted less than an hour.*

finally to flee into India and China. When the monsoon rains came in May, the Japanese paused to consolidate their positions. By then, the banner of Japan's rising sun flew over most of Burma.

Japan's Defensive Perimeter

In May 1942, the seemingly unstoppable Japanese conquerors, in accord with their Kodo-inspired master strategy, dominated most of Southeast Asia. The emperor's warriors had successfully eliminated Western influence in the Greater East Asia Co-Prosperity Sphere in less than six months. And they had established a defensive perimeter that stretched southeast from the Kurile Islands to the Marshall and Gilbert Islands, west through parts of the Solomon Islands and New Guinea, southward encircling the Netherlands East Indies (now the Republic of Indonesia), then northwest in a great arc around Sumatra to India. The swing of the arc included the Southern Regions, rich in oil and raw material. And just to the south of the perimeter lay the Coral Sea and Australia.

Battle of the Coral Sea

After nearly six months of continuous naval action in the waters of Southeast Asia, a growing number of Japanese admirals favored a temporary halt in the offensive. They pointed out the need for resting navy personnel and repairing damaged vessels. But Japanese naval strategists with the ultimate authority to establish policy thought otherwise.

As the first step toward totally occupying the Solomons and New Guinea, Japan's war planners ordered the invasion of Tulagi in the southern Solomons and Port Moresby, Papua (geographically part of New Guinea). Consolidating the southernmost section of Japan's defensive perimeter would further isolate Australia and prepare the way for the eventual conquest of the Australian continent.

On May 3, 1942, the Japanese seized Tulagi and started building a seaplane base. The next day, a Japanese invasion fleet of some twenty-seven vessels left Rabaul, New Guinea, and steamed southward into the Coral Sea, its course set for Port Moresby. The Japanese fleet included the carrier *Shoho*. A two-carrier American task force rushed to intercept the Port Moresby invasion fleet. In turn, a two-carrier Japanese battle group proceeded at full-ahead speed to head off the American task force.

Beginning on May 7, the Battle of the Coral Sea raged for two days. It was the first naval battle in history to be fought entirely by aircraft. No surface ships either saw or contacted one another throughout the engagement. The battle ended in a draw: The Japanese gained a tactical victory, but the Americans won a strategic decision.

Both sides, however, rushed to claim total victory. On May 9, 1942, the *New York Times* proclaimed:

JAPANESE REPULSED IN GREAT PACIFIC BATTLE, WITH 17 TO 22 OF THEIR SHIPS SUNK OR CRIPPLED: ENEMY IN FLIGHT, PURSUED BY ALLIED WARSHIPS

An article in the *Japan Times & Advertiser* recounted the battle in hardly less glowing terms: "The effect of the terrible setback in the Coral Sea is indeed beyond description. A state of mania is prevalent in the American munitions field."

The truth lay somewhere in between these exaggerations: Highlighting the American losses was the sinking of the much-loved carrier *Lexington*—the "Lady Lex." The other American carrier, *Yorktown*, survived the battle but took a bomb hit that killed sixty-six crew members. A destroyer and a tanker were also lost. Japanese losses included one carrier sunk, the *Shoho*, and another carrier badly damaged, the *Shokaku*. A third carrier, the *Zuikaku*, suffered no damage. But the Japanese lost two-thirds of its carrier planes and half its airmen.

Tactically, in terms of raw tonnage sunk, the Japanese could honestly claim victory in the Coral Sea encounter. Strategically, in that the Japanese were denied a foothold in Port Moresby and thereby prevented from further expansion to the south, the Americans clearly came away winners in the first great naval air battle.

Survivors from a burning USS Lexington *climb aboard a U.S. ship following the Battle of the Coral Sea on May 8, 1942.*

Perhaps the most important aspect of the Coral Sea clash lay in the postbattle status of the participating aircraft carriers. The damage to the *Shokaku* required two months to repair. It took nearly that long to replace *Zuikaku*'s lost aircraft. Despite severe bomb damage to the *Yorktown*, however, repairs to the U.S. vessel were completed within weeks of the Coral Sea battle.

In less than a month, the two navies would clash again, harder. Neither *Shokaku* nor *Zuikaku* would be ready for action. *Yorktown* would. And *Yorktown* would make all the difference.

Japan's rising sun had reached its apex high over the wide Pacific and was starting to cast long shadows eastward. Those shadows would soon fall darkly on the white sands of Midway Atoll.

The Americans succeeded in sinking the Japanese carrier Shoho *during the Battle of the Coral Sea.*

CHAPTER ONE

How It Began

"After June of this year we should occupy Midway, Johnston, and Palmyra, send our air force forward to these islands and dispatch the Combined Fleet with an occupying force to occupy Hawaii and at the same time bring the enemy fleet into decisive battle."
>   —*Rear Admiral Matome Ugaki*
>   chief of staff to Admiral Isoroku Yamamoto,
>   commander in chief, Combined Japanese Fleet
>   Diary entry, January 1942

After the enormously successful attack on Pearl Harbor, and the string of quick victories that followed, Japan's military commanders soon found themselves facing a vital planning decision: Should they dig in and bolster their present, fairly easily won positions? Or should they continue advancing and extending their ever-widening defensive perimeter?

Mitsuo Fuchida and Masatake Okumiya, who took part in the Battle of Midway as naval aviators, indicate the reasoning used by their countrymen in plotting Japan's next moves:

At the start of the Pacific War, Japan's strategy-makers had been so engrossed in the immediate problem of acquiring oil resources that they had formulated no concrete strategic program for the ensuing course of hostilities after these resources had been won.

Also, they had been keenly conscious of the many risks involved in the initial operations—the Pearl Harbor attack not the least of such risks—and had by no means been certain of the outcome. They therefore had decided to wait and see how the operations progressed before attempting to formulate subsequent war strategy.

Admiral Isoroku Yamamoto, the wily commander of Japan's Combined Fleet, favored continuing the offensive. It would court disaster, he felt, to allow time for the industrial might of America to kick in and enable the Allies to reclaim all that Japan had gained. Yamamoto wanted to press the limits of Japan's success by attacking Midway and the Aleutian Islands. The Army General Staff preferred to stick with original Japanese plans for holding and developing positions along their established defensive perimeter. The debate that followed lasted well into spring.

Japanese Chain of Command

In theory, responsibility for planning Japan's strategic policy belonged to the general staffs of the army and the navy. Both staffs operated as sections of Imperial General Headquarters. The Chief of Naval General Staff was also Chief of the Navy Section, which issued top-level orders and directives to the commander in chief of the Combined Fleet. In January 1942, Admiral Isoroku Yamamoto held the office of commander in chief, Combined Fleet.

Admiral Isoroku Yamamoto was often at odds with other Japanese strategists over the plan of attack following Pearl Harbor.

Yamamoto, perhaps the most loved and respected among all Japan's admirals, brought another dimension to his office. The reverential treatment he received from his superiors, peers, and juniors alike enabled him to exert a strong, often decisive force on strategic policy planning at the highest levels. A case in point can be found in Japan's decision to attack Pearl Harbor.

Yamamoto personally planned the Pearl Harbor attack. When the Naval General Staff opposed his plan, Yamamoto threatened to resign his commission unless the Staff relented and approved it. The Staff quickly withdrew its opposition and the plan went forward. Yamamoto's influence increased dramatically after his resounding success at Pearl Harbor. And his staff at Combined Fleet Headquarters fairly bubbled with self-confidence and enthusiasm.

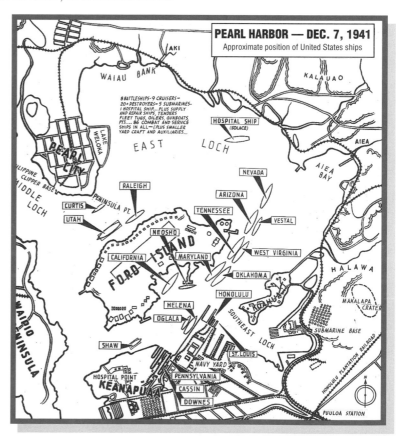

Primary responsibility and final approval for all naval planning rested with the Naval General Staff. The hugely successful Pearl Harbor attack plan, however, had been designed by Yamamoto and his Combined Fleet staff. In light of Yamamoto's earlier success, members of the Naval General Staff now felt reluctant to interfere further either with the admiral or with his staff. Thus the initiative for planning the next phase of the naval war then fell quite naturally to Yamamoto's colleagues of the Combined Fleet.

Second-Term Strategy

In January 1942, Yamamoto summoned his chief of staff, Rear Admiral Matome Ugaki, and ordered him "to plan second term strategy at once." Yamamoto's "at once" phrasing suggested an urgency perhaps fostered by his sense that by then second-phase planning should have already been in place.

Ugaki began work at once. He estimated that Japan's first-phase offensive operations would conclude about mid-March. This meant that subsequent offensive actions must be decided on no later than the end of February. Ugaki then "spent four days in quiet and exhaustive deliberation" on board his flagship *Nagato*, anchored in Hiroshima Bay. He considered three alternatives for a second major offensive move: south toward Australia; west toward Ceylon and India; or back to Hawaii to occupy the islands and complete the destruction of the U.S. Pacific Fleet. He settled on Hawaii.

Ugaki completed a preliminary plan and sent it to his staff for review. They promptly concluded that an attack on Hawaii would not work for three reasons. First, Japan could not count on surprising the Americans as they had on December 7. Second, available Japanese air strength was insufficient for maintaining control of the air. And third, the odds would favor the Americans in a battle between Japanese ships and American shore batteries. Ugaki then directed his staff to draft an alternative plan that had been suggested by one of his staff officers.

Senior fleet operations officer Captain Kameto Kuroshima proposed continuing offensive operations toward Ceylon and India in the west. By capturing Ceylon, Kuroshima hoped to safeguard the already occupied Dutch East Indies and Malaya against Allied attack. But when the Army General Staff complained that it could not commit enough troops to support the operation, Kuroshima's plan was also scrapped.

Yamamoto's Combined Fleet planners next proposed a move against Midway Atoll in the east, a somewhat watered-down version of Ugaki's Hawaii plan. Midway would provide Japan with a base from which to eventually launch an attack on Hawaii. At the same time, Combined Fleet hoped to lure the remaining American fleet into a decisive sea battle that would hasten an end to the war. At this point, however, the Naval General Staff introduced a plan of its own, recommending a southward advance.

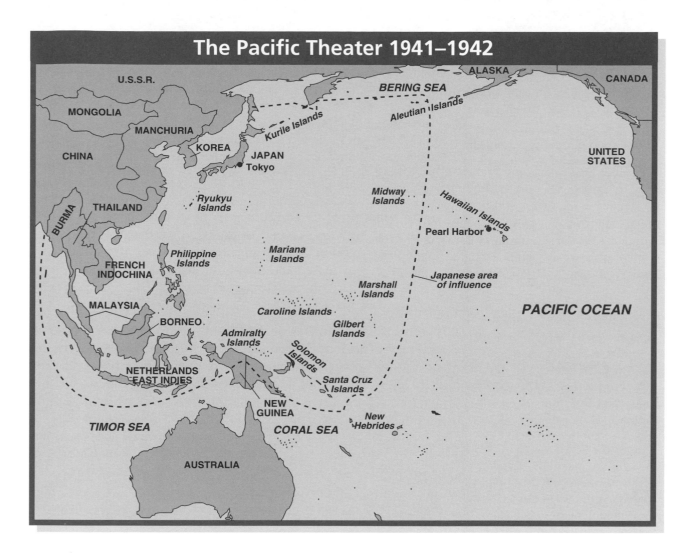

The Pacific Theater 1941–1942

The Naval General Staff wanted to make it impossible for the Allies to launch a future counteroffensive from Australia. But again the Army General Staff cited the inability of its service to support such a large-scale operation. The Naval General Staff then countered with a plan to cut Australia's supply lines by gradually extending Japan's control over New Guinea, the Solomons, and the New Caledonia–Fiji Islands area. (Preparations to consolidate Japanese positions in New Guinea and the Solomons—leading to the Battle of the Coral Sea—were in fact already under way.)

Breaking the Deadlock

Yamamoto immediately opposed the southward move and threw his full support into the Midway plan prepared by his own staff. More haggling ensued. The army indicated that it could muster enough troops to support Yamamoto's feint in the Aleutians. The issue was finally settled on April 5.

Doolittle's Raid

On April 18, 1942, the U.S. Army Air Corps brought the war home to the Japanese in a daring air raid on Tokyo. Sixteen North American B-25 Mitchell bombers, commanded by Lieutenant Colonel James H. "Jimmy" Doolittle, bombed Tokyo and other Japanese cities, catching the Japanese by complete surprise.

Doolittle's attack originated from the U.S. aircraft carrier *Hornet*, which formed a part of Vice Admiral William F. "Bull" Halsey's *Enterprise* task force. The B-25s flew eight hundred miles to their targets. They inflicted little physical damage but delivered a severe blow to Japanese morale. American spirits, badly in need of an uplift, soared over news of the attack.

Fifteen of the attacking planes were lost or forced to crash land in China. One B-25 landed in Vladivostok, where the crew and plane were interned by the Soviets, who had not yet entered the war on the side of the Allies. Most of Doolittle's airmen survived, but two fell captive to the Japanese and were beheaded.

Besides boosting American morale, the Doolittle raid served to hurry along the Japanese high command in its decision to expand Japan's defensive perimeter by attacking Midway.

At a joint meeting of the Naval General Staff and the Combined Fleet staff, Commander Yasuji Watanabe read a message in which Yamamoto stated his position in no uncertain terms: "In the last analysis, the success or failure of our entire strategy in the Pacific will be determined by whether or not we succeed in destroying the United States Fleet, more particularly its carrier forces." The message pointed out that the best way to cut Australia's supply lines was to destroy the U.S. carrier force. Without the carriers, the supply lines could not exist. Yamamoto's staff concluded by stating:

We believe that by launching the proposed operations against Midway, we can succeed in drawing out the enemy's carrier strength and destroying it in a decisive battle. If, on the other hand, the enemy should avoid our challenge, we shall still realize an important gain by advancing our defensive perimeter to Midway and the western Aleutians without obstruction.

The Naval General Staff conferred briefly. To break the deadlock they reluctantly agreed to support the Midway plan. The respected and revered Yamamoto had prevailed once again. Yet, even after agreeing in principle to the Midway operation, the General Staff continued to argue over how and when to set the plan in motion. Then chance took a hand to end all debate.

On April 18, 1942, a special attack squadron of sixteen American B-25 "Mitchell" medium bombers, led by Colonel James H. Doolittle, bombed Tokyo and other major Japanese cities. Flying

The B-25 bombers flown by James Doolittle's squadron on board the flight deck of the USS Hornet *en route to the raid's launching point. Doolittle's raid on Japanese cities, while causing little physical damage, caused emotional turmoil as the Japanese realized that they, too, were vulnerable to attack.*

Jimmy Doolittle's Tokyo bombing crew and some Chinese friends after the U.S. airmen bailed out following their famous air raid on Japan.

off the U.S. carrier *Hornet*, the B-25s inflicted little tactical damage, but their bombs raised havoc with Japanese morale. Fleet operations officer Kuroshima said that "it passed like a shiver over Japan." A next-day editorial in the Japanese newspaper *Nichi Nichi* warned:

> Although this was Japan's first experience of a hostile air raid, the nation must be prepared for a frequent recurrence of similar incidents hereafter. On the assumption that future raids will be more violent and on a larger scale, the nation must form a firmer determination to meet them with calm and confidence.

Operation MI

With the Japanese capital shown to be open to enemy attack, all the bickering over strategy ceased at once. The Midway plan—from then on called Operation MI—proceeded at full-ahead speed.

On April 29, Yamamoto held a meeting with his ranking officers on board the *Yamato*, recently named as his flagship. Captain Kuroshima—called "the God of Operations" by his fellow officers—had by then developed Yamamoto's basic plan into a detailed war plan involving nearly two hundred ships. The operation would range over a watery battle course of 2,000 miles, stretching from the Aleutians to Midway, some 2,300 miles east of the Japanese home islands. During a review of Kuroshima's planning, not everyone displayed optimism toward the coming venture. According to one well-placed observer, Commander Minoru Genda, Vice Admiral Chuichi Nagumo's attitude was "not so definite." But the general atmosphere was one of great confidence.

Rear Admiral Ryunosuke Kusaka, First Air Fleet chief of staff under Nagumo, recalled that Kuroshima's plan had been accepted without any arm-twisting. "We Japanese slighted the strength of Americans and got self-conceited because of easy successes in the first stage of operations," he said. "In other words, we thought that the enemy could be easily destroyed even if it did come out to meet us in force."

Yamamoto, perhaps sensing a mood of overconfidence, ended the meeting with a warning: "Unless more efforts based upon long-range planning are put into military preparations and operations, it will be very hard to win the final victory. It is like a disease to think that an invincible status has been achieved after being satisfied with the past successful operations."

During May, Yamamoto assembled every available ship in the Japanese navy: 11 battleships, 8 carriers, 23 cruisers, 65 destroyers, 21 submarines, and scores of auxiliary ships—a total of 190 ships. In addition to the naval vessels, approximately 700 aircraft formed a part of Yamamoto's battle (or tactical) force. It represented the largest fleet yet put together in the Pacific.

Of the armada's size, Fuchida and Okumiya later wrote: "The ships participating were to consume more fuel and cover a greater mileage in this one operation than the peacetime Japanese Navy had ever done in an entire year."

Yamamoto's Tactical Forces

The command structure for Operation MI, under the overall command of Admiral Isoroku Yamamoto, comprised six major tactical forces. Listed by name and responsible commander, they were as follows.

1. MAIN FORCE; Admiral Isoroku Yamamoto. The main force consisted of three battleships, a light carrier, cruisers, destroyers, and seaplane carriers. They were to be positioned about six hundred miles northwest of Midway. From there they could aid, as needed, either the Midway or the Northern (Aleutian) attacking forces.

2. FIRST CARRIER STRIKING FORCE; Vice Admiral Chuichi Nagumo. The striking force comprised four carriers, with added screening and support groups of battleships, cruisers, and destroyers. The primary mission of Nagumo's force was to destroy American defenses at Midway. Beyond that, Nagumo was to engage and destroy the American fleet if it appeared on scene.

3. MIDWAY INVASION FORCE; Vice Admiral Nobutake Kondo. Kondo's force was made up of a main body of battle-

ships, cruisers, and destroyers; a close support group of cruisers and destroyers; a transport group of troop transports, cruisers, and destroyers; a seaplane tender group; and a minesweeper group. Their assignment was to invade and occupy Midway Atoll.

4. NORTHERN (ALEUTIAN) FORCE; Vice Admiral Moshiro Hosogaya. Hosogaya's mission was to provide a diversionary strike against American installations at Dutch Harbor in the Aleutians and to invade and occupy the islands of Attu and Kiska. In addition to a two-carrier striking force, his battle group included a main body of one cruiser and two destroyers, separate Attu and Kiska invasion forces, and a submarine detachment. With Hosogayo's northward feint, Yamamoto hoped to lure the U.S. fleet away from Midway.

5. ADVANCE (SUBMARINE) FORCE; Vice Admiral Teruhisa Komatsu. The Advance Force of two submarine tenders and fifteen submarines was to fan out northwest of Hawaii and provide Yamamoto with advance information about U.S. fleet movements into and out of Pearl Harbor. (Komatsu's submarines arrived late on station and failed to observe the departure of the American task forces from Pearl Harbor.)

6. SHORE-BASED AIR FORCE; Vice Admiral Nishizo Tsukahara. Tsukahara's air force consisted of an expeditionary force, an air flotilla, and two air groups, which comprised 108 fighters, 72 torpedo bombers, 10 land bombers, and 24 flying boats. They were assigned the task of establishing an advanced air base at Midway after Japanese troops had secured the atoll. From Midway, they intended to mount air attacks on the Hawaiian Islands.

Vice Admiral Nishizo Tsukahara led the Japanese shore-based air force. (Below) A photo shows a group of Japanese naval aviators. This print was developed from film taken from a Japanese prisoner captured on the island of Attu.

Winning Hands Down

While Yamamoto assembled his fleet for Operation MI, the Battle of the Coral Sea was being fought. Since Yamamoto intended to use every available ship in the navy, some ships then in the Coral Sea were expected to join his Midway fleet later. The original MI plan included the carriers *Shokaku* and *Zuikaku*. But on May 17, *Shokaku* returned to Japan from the Coral Sea with its flight deck badly bent. Two days later, *Zuikaku* arrived home with its aircraft squadrons all but destroyed. Neither carrier could be made ready in time for the Midway strike and had to be dropped from the striking force.

The loss of one-third of his carrier strength did not overly concern Yamamoto. Japanese intelligence had reported the sinking of U.S. carriers *Yorktown* and *Lexington* in the Coral Sea. (In fact, *Yorktown* not only was not sunk but would return to service. In addition, the Japanese actually reported *Saratoga* sunk rather than *Lexington*, but this was an error: *Saratoga*, which had been torpedoed by a Japanese submarine five hundred miles off Oahu on January 11, was in Bremerton, Washington, for repairs.) A more recent intelligence report indicated further that U.S. carriers *Enterprise* and *Hornet* had been rushed to the South Pacific to replace *Yorktown* and *Lexington*. Yamamoto felt fairly certain that his fleet would be unopposed by American carriers at Midway. The absence of American carriers would all but guarantee the success of Operation MI.

The Second World War, especially the war in the Pacific, saw the end of the battleship's reign as "queen of battle" on the high seas. Whereas the range of a battleship's guns was limited to a

Dive-bombers return to an aircraft carrier after completing a mission.

Kamikaze!

American carrier-based aircraft eventually grew into a powerfully destructive and dominating force in the Pacific war. Japan, in desperation, resorted to suicide squadrons known as the *Kamikaze* (Special Attack) Corps to lash back at the Americans.

Kamikaze means "divine wind" in Japanese. The corps's name recalled the legend of Ise, the Japanese wind god. Ise supposedly caused the typhoon that destroyed Kublai Khan's invasion fleet in 1281, saving Japan from Mongol rule. By deliberately smashing their bomb-laden planes into U.S. ships without hope of survival, Japanese pilots hoped to stem the American advance and spare their home islands from invasion.

The *kamikaze* suicide attacks began in Leyte Gulf in the Philippines in October 1944. They continued until shortly before the war ended nearly a year later. The *kamikazes* damaged or sank a total of 322 Allied vessels during this period.

A Japanese proverb asserts: *Life is as the weight of a feather compared to one's duty.* Twelve hundred and twenty-eight uncommonly valiant pilots of the "divine wind" joined their honored ancestors, holding unflinchingly to duty's creed.

A kamikaze *just misses its target, plummeting past the catwalk of the USS* Sangamon *into the sea after being hit by antiaircraft fire. During the final days of World War II, desperate Japanese resorted to more* kamikaze *attacks.*

Japan Rules the Waves

The Japanese celebrate May 27 as Navy Day, honoring the anniversary date of Admiral Heihachiro Togo's great victory over the Russians at Tsushima in 1905. The Japanese press never missed a chance to praise its great and glorious navy. On May 27, 1942, as elements of Yamamoto's Combined Fleet departed Japanese ports and headed for Midway, the *Japan Times and Advertiser* continued the tradition:

> This year, Navy Day is not a day of mere remembrance, not a mere reminder; it is a day of fulfillment. The Japanese Navy has not only duplicated the exploits of 37 years ago, but it has repeated it [sic] time and again and on an unbelievably greater scale....This is the moment of culmination [high point], the moment of fulfillment.
>
> Today, Britain's control over the seas has vanished, thanks to the work of the German and Italian submarines and more to the work of the Japanese Navy. Britain's auxiliary, the United States, has likewise had her navy practically destroyed by the Japanese Navy. As a result, Japan stands today as the premier naval Power of the world. It may well presage the rise of Japan in the future history of the world to a position comparable to that which Britain has occupied in the past.

maximum of about twenty-six miles, airplanes launched from aircraft carriers—the new queens of battle—could deliver their lethal loads on targets *hundreds* of miles distant. Naval warfare had entered an age in which entire battles were fought without the opponents' ships ever drawing within sight of one another. Victory at sea had become a case of the navy with the most carriers in any given battle most often winning the fight.

After six months of amazing success, "victory fever" had possessed Yamamoto, as it had most Japanese. Despite the loss of *Shokaku* and *Zuikaku*, he felt convinced that he and his four remaining carriers were unbeatable.

Rear Admiral Kusaka echoed Yamamoto's confidence, indicating that losing two carriers from their strike force really did not matter: "We can beat the Yankees hands down with a single blow."

Eastward Toward the Rising Sun

Operation MI commenced during the last week of May, with the attack on Midway now firmly set for June 4.

Rear Admiral Kakuji Kakuta's Second Carrier Striking Force (part of the Northern Force) hauled anchor out of Ominato harbor at noon on May 26 and charted a course eastward toward the Aleutians. Kakuta's planes were scheduled to mount a diversionary attack—a feint—against Dutch Harbor on June 3, just prior to the main attack at Midway.

The next day, the principal component of Operation MI, Vice Admiral Chuichi Nagumo's First Carrier Striking Force, departed Hashirajima. (Hashirajima, an island just south of Hiroshima in the Inland Sea, had served as safe harbor and headquarters for the Combined Fleet since the start of the war.) Responsibility rested with Nagumo and his striking force, the *Kido Butai*, for the ultimate success or failure at Midway.

After Nagumo's departure, Vice Admiral Moshiro Hosogaya's main Northern Force left Japan for the Aleutians on May 28. That evening, Rear Admiral Raizo Tanaka's Transport Group (part of the Midway Invasion Force) with five thousand invasion troops set sail for Midway out of Saipan, one of the Mariana Islands southeast of Japan. They were escorted by a light cruiser, a tanker, and a shielding force of four cruisers.

The last two units slipped moorings in Japan's Inland Sea on the following morning and proceeded through the Bungo Straits, heading southeasterly into the Pacific Ocean. They comprised the sixteen warships of the Midway Invasion Force, commanded by Vice Admiral Nobutake Kondo; and, last, the thirty-two warships of Isoroku Yamamoto's Main Force, including his flagship *Yamato*, the giant battleship that carried the name for old Japan.

As his huge armada steamed eastward toward the rising sun, Yamamoto beamed with confidence, secure in the knowledge that he would soon oversee the total destruction of the American fleet. He would once again surprise the unsuspecting Americans, just as he had at Pearl Harbor. A great Japanese victory at Midway would break the American spirit and win the war for Japan.

Yamamoto knew that secrecy was vital to Japanese success at Midway. He felt sure that secrecy had been strictly preserved. Paragraph (d) of Admiral Nagumo's latest intelligence estimate had reaffirmed that "The enemy is not aware of our plans." Yamamoto could almost taste the fruits of victory.

He had no way of knowing that the Americans were aware of his movements and attack plans. Or that they were preparing even then to greet him at a grid location about 325 miles northeast of Midway. The point from which the Americans hoped to surprise Yamamoto's fleet bore the hopeful name of Point Luck.

Unknown to Yamamoto and the other Japanese, U.S. cryptographers in Washington, D.C., had broken the Japanese secret code shortly before the attack on Pearl Harbor. This good work enabled the Americans to learn of the Midway invasion plan well in advance of its execution. The key element of surprise belonged not to the Japanese but to the Americans. This advantage was gratefully accepted by Admiral Chester W. Nimitz, commander in chief of the U.S. Pacific Fleet (CinCPAC) at Pearl Harbor. But would the advantage be sufficient to overcome the mighty armada then gathering against him?

Nimitz faced the impending defense of Midway armed with a slingshot and not too many rocks. To provide a proper welcome for Yamamoto's huge fleet, Nimitz could put together only a cluster of 27 ships of the line—3 carriers, 6 heavy cruisers, a light cruiser, 17 destroyers—and 233 carrier-based aircraft. Army, navy, and marine land-based planes on Midway upped the total to 348 available aircraft. But Chester Nimitz was not a man to flinch when the going turned tough.

Admiral Chester Nimitz took over command of the U.S. Pacific Fleet when morale was low and the fleet had suffered considerable damage.

Nimitz Takes Command

Admiral Nimitz, a former submariner, assumed command of the U.S. Pacific Fleet in Pearl Harbor on December 31, 1941, replacing Admiral Husband E. Kimmel, who had commanded the fleet before and during the Japanese attack on December 7. The change of command ceremony took place aboard the submarine *Grayling*. Nimitz had worked long and hard for such an appointment, but it was not the best time ever to take charge of the Pacific Fleet.

Earlier, Nimitz had displayed misgivings when breaking the news of the appointment to his wife. "I'm the new commander in chief," he said without enthusiasm. She sensed his distress and quickly said, "You've wanted this all your life."

The admiral's reply, however, reflected his concern: "But sweetheart, all the ships are at the bottom." A slight exaggeration but understandable under the circumstances.

The new fleet commander was not one to dwell on ill fortune, however. He set right to work improving morale among the personnel and salvaging his fleet. Those who served under Nimitz would soon recognize his fine leadership qualities, as did Rear Admiral Raymond A. Spruance, who was to play a principal role at Midway.

When Nimitz assumed command of the Pacific Fleet, Spruance said, "It was like being in a stuffy room and having someone open a window and let in a breath of fresh air." Spruance respected Nimitz totally:

> Nimitz combined so many fine qualities that you could not put your finger on any one of them and say, "Here is the key to the man." The one big thing about him was that he was always ready to fight. . . . And he wanted officers who would push the fight against the Japanese. If they would not do so, they were sent elsewhere.

By the middle of May, Nimitz knew enough about Operation MI to realize that he was about to face the greatest fight of his naval career. Most of his information came from Commander Joseph J. Rochefort Jr. Rochefort had helped crack the top Japanese naval code JN-25 in 1940. He now headed the navy's combat intelligence office at Pearl Harbor.

Rochefort's group received daily intelligence reports on Japanese activities from U.S. codebreakers in Washington. In addition, his people continually monitored the airwaves for coded Japanese transmissions, which they promptly decoded and passed on to their chief. Rochefort in turn informed Admiral Nimitz of Japanese intentions and movements on a moment-by-moment basis. Few officers under Nimitz affected the outcome at Midway more than Commander Rochefort.

Nimitz began assembling his forces at once. He called in Vice Admiral William F. "Bull" Halsey's Task Force 16 from the South Pacific, where it had arrived too late to take part in the Coral Sea battle. He ordered the crippled *Yorktown* back to Pearl Harbor at the same time. Meanwhile, the navy broadcast fake radio messages to make the Japanese think that the carriers *Enterprise* and *Hornet* (part of Task Force 16) remained in southern waters.

Commander Joseph J. Rochefort and his intelligence group helped crack a top secret Japanese naval code and provided valuable information to Nimitz.

American Task Forces

Late in May, Nimitz divided his defending forces three ways. He first sent Task Force 8, under Rear Admiral Robert A. Theobold, to deal with Hosogaya's Aleutian feint. He next assigned Rear Admiral Spruance to command Task Force 16 aboard *Enterprise*, replacing Bull Halsey, who had been hospitalized for shingles, a severe skin disorder brought on by overwork and stress. Spruance, Halsey's former cruiser commander, had been recommended to Nimitz by the ailing admiral. Nimitz completed his assignments by naming Rear Admiral Frank Jack Fletcher to lead Task Force 17 aboard *Yorktown* and, as senior ranking officer, to assume overall command of both Midway-bound task forces. Restoring the badly damaged *Yorktown* to fighting trim at Pearl Harbor in only forty-eight hours of around-the-clock repairs stands as one of Midway's "minor" miracles.

Nimitz directed Fletcher and Spruance to take up positions northeast of Midway, outside the range of Japanese carrier-based search planes. The longer range (seven hundred miles) of U.S. land-based reconnaissance planes from Midway would enable them to find the enemy carriers before the Japanese drew within sighting range of the U.S. carriers. By becoming first to sight the enemy, Fletcher and Spruance would gain a leg up.

USS Yorktown *is readied for the Battle of Midway.*

Before his task force commanders departed, Nimitz also issued a letter of instructions to them. The document reflected his concern over the need to preserve U.S. carriers in the face of a larger enemy force. Unless far greater losses were inflicted upon the Japanese, any further American carrier losses would severely cripple America's ability to continue challenging Japan's navy in the Pacific. Thus Nimitz warned of the impending risks.

> In carrying out the task assigned . . . you will be governed by the principle of calculated risk, which you shall interpret to mean avoidance of exposure of your force to attack by superior enemy forces without good prospect of inflicting as a result of such exposure, greater damage on the enemy.

It then became time for others to act.

Spruance's Task Force 16 weighed anchor out of Pearl Harbor on May 28, followed two days later by Fletcher's Task Force 17. Meanwhile, Theobold's Task Force 8 steamed north to Alaskan waters, where it would engage Hosogaya's Northern Force on June 3. Far to the south, one of the most decisive sea battles in history—if not *the* most decisive battle—would begin the next day.

CHAPTER TWO

First Strike

"I noted that Nagumo had changed, and I began to feel dissatisfied with his apparent conservatism and passiveness. It might have been because he was now commanding an air arm, which was not his specialty . . . but his once-vigorous fighting spirit seemed to be gone, and with it his stature as an outstanding naval leader. Instead he seemed rather average, and I was suddenly aware of his increased age."

—Air Unit Commander Mitsuo I. Fuchida,
speaking of Vice Admiral Chuichi Nagumo,
commander, First Carrier Striking Force

Midway lies about 1,150 miles northwest of Hawaii. The main islets of the Midway Atoll are Sand and Eastern; Sand Island, less than two miles long and half as wide, is the larger. The U.S. Navy claimed that "an air base at Midway Island is second in importance only to Pearl Harbor." In reality, however, Midway was known for little more than its use as a way station for the famed China Clipper—one of the four-engined flying boats that established the first trans-Pacific air route in the mid-1930s. But because of Midway's nearness to Hawaii, Yamamoto reasoned, the Americans could not allow an enemy to occupy it. The United States would therefore risk its entire available fleet to defend this tiny atoll in the wide Pacific. The success of Yamamoto's strategy hinged on that premise.

Yamamoto's rather complex battle plan for Operation MI was separated into four phases. First, Hosogaya's Northern Force was

Melancholy Midway

A roughly circular coral reef defines the limits of Midway Atoll and forms a tropical lagoon about five miles across. The two main islands (islets), Sand and Eastern, lie just inside the reef to the south. In surface area, Sand Island measures about 850 acres. Eastern Island is something less than half that size. Both islands are flat, arid, and overrun with gooney birds (petrel). The atoll's strategic importance derives solely from its location "midway" across the Pacific.

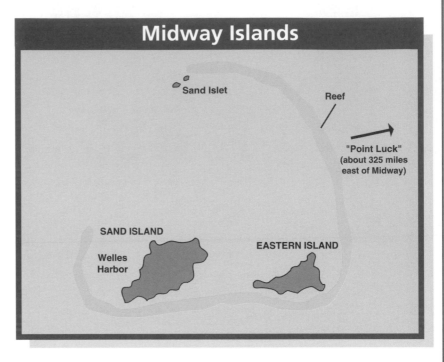

Midway Islands

Sand Islet

Reef

"Point Luck"
(about 325 miles
east of Midway)

SAND ISLAND

Welles
Harbor

EASTERN ISLAND

In 1891, George A. Munro, a scientist with the Rothschild Expedition, put in to Midway aboard the British sailing vessel *Wandering Minstrel*. In the diary he kept during his brief stay, Munro noted that Sand Island is "almost a mile long, low and sandy, with a few mounds 12 feet high covered with large scrub at one end; at the other end is a patch of grass.

"It is a very desolate island," the scientist reported, "with a great extent of low-lying sandy ground, which seems to be swept by heavy seas during heavy weather. . . . There is something melancholy about this desolate place. The sigh of the wind 'round the house, the wail of the petrel, at any time melancholy, seems even more so . . . a feeling of depression comes over me."

to launch an assault against the Aleutians to divert the U.S. fleet away from Midway. Second, carrier-based aircraft from Nagumo's First Carrier Striking Force would mount a bombing attack on Midway the next day to neutralize American defenses on the atoll. Third, five thousand troops of Kondo's Midway Invasion Force would follow up with an amphibious landing to secure the airfield on Eastern Island. And fourth, after the capture of Midway, Yamamoto's Main Force would join Nagumo's unit in heading off and destroying the U.S. fleet as it rushed from the Aleutians to defend Midway.

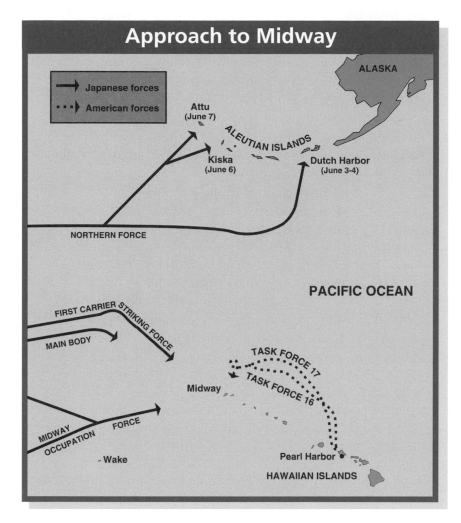

Approach to Midway

Japanese forces →
American forces ···▶

ALASKA

Attu
(June 7)

ALEUTIAN ISLANDS

Kiska
(June 6)

Dutch Harbor
(June 3-4)

NORTHERN FORCE

PACIFIC OCEAN

FIRST CARRIER STRIKING FORCE

MAIN BODY

TASK FORCE 17

TASK FORCE 16

Midway

MIDWAY OCCUPATION FORCE

Wake

Pearl Harbor

HAWAIIAN ISLANDS

The plan looked great on paper. However, it relied on the Americans to do exactly what Yamamoto expected them to do. And Yamamoto had not expected Nimitz to have advance knowledge of the Japanese scheme.

Aleutian Assault

True to Yamamoto's grand strategy, Admiral Hosogaya's Northern Force outmaneuvered Admiral Theobold's Task Force 8 (which consisted mainly of cruisers) and struck on schedule in the Aleutians. Theobold had assumed, not illogically, that the Japanese would fake an invasion attempt at Attu and Kiska and then attack the more important American base at Dutch Harbor, farther east on Unalaska Island. Therefore he positioned his ships close to Dutch Harbor, allowing the Japanese to land unopposed to the west at Attu and Kiska, two tiny islands that appeared to offer minimal strategic value. It was later learned, however, that the Japanese believed that the Americans might try to invade Japan's home islands from Attu and Kiska.

The Japanese attack Dutch Harbor on Unalaska Island on June 3, 1942. The bombs set a tank farm on fire that damaged a radio station.

On both June 3 and June 4, planes from the carriers *Ryujo* and *Junyo* bombed Dutch Harbor. Hosogaya, while avoiding attacks by American land-based aircraft from various Alaskan locations, managed to land small forces on the islands of Kiska and Attu on June 6 and June 7, respectively. The Japanese gains resulted in little more than an embarrassment to U.S. military commanders over the loss of two isolated islands of small strategic worth.

As might be expected, though, the landings set American imaginations to wondering whether the Japanese might strike next at Hawaii or the U.S. mainland. A Honolulu *Star-Bulletin* editorial cautioned that "Dutch Harbor may be an isolated raid or it may be part of a series of attacks all along the Pacific coast and upon Hawaii."

While Japan's attack on the Aleutians managed to provoke a flurry of far-fetched American imaginings, Hosogaya's Northern Force failed to divert the main U.S. fleet from Midway.

Hitting the Jackpot

Although armed with advance knowledge of Yamamoto's planned attacks on Midway and the Aleutians, Admiral Nimitz could not be sure which projected move was the feint and which was the main thrust. Even as Task Forces 16 and 17 arrived at Point Luck on June 2, Nimitz could not be positive that Midway represented the main event. The situation developed into a giant guessing game of huge consequence. Nimitz guessed right. On June 2, he sent a message to all ships at sea in his task forces:

Secrets of the Zero

Perhaps the most far-reaching effect of Japan's attack on the Aleutians grew out of Flight Petty Officer Tadayoshi Koga's forced landing on tiny Akutan Island, east of Dutch Harbor. Although the aircraft suffered only minor damage, Koga, the pilot, struck his head on impact and did not survive the crash. Jiro Horikoshi, designer of the famous Zero fighter, explained later.

In the Aleutian operation, which was conducted simultaneously [with the Midway operation] and was reported to be a success much greater than it actually was, an unfortunate incident occurred. An almost undamaged Zero made a forced landing on an uninhabited island and the United States took possession of it. There was not a single person in Japan at the time who knew about this. Since Pearl Harbor, the United States had made many efforts to discover the secrets of our mysterious airplane, including an attempt to assemble pieces of downed aircraft into one flyable model. Now the Americans were able to conduct an investigation of Japan's newest fighter from all angles, using this almost perfect model for flight tests. They quickly learned the advantages and disadvantages of the Zero. The results of their investigation played a significant role in new fighter design and tactics to be used against our fighters.

The Japanese Zero was almost unbeatable in speed and maneuverability. Shown below is a captured Zero wearing U.S. insignia.

Denying the Enemy Surprise

Ensign Jewell H. "Jack" Reid flew his Catalina flying boat out of the Midway lagoon at 0415 on June 3. At 0900, Reid became the first person to spot the enemy, sighting a large number of Japanese ships about seven hundred miles southwest of Midway. His early sighting of the enemy came as no accident.

Rear Admiral Patrick N.L. Bellinger, Commander Patrol Wings Hawaiian Area, bore responsibility for reconnaissance flights out of Midway. In an earlier planning conference with Admiral Nimitz, Bellinger said, "The problem is one of hitting before we are hit."

"To deny the enemy surprise, our search must ensure discovery of his carriers before they launch their first attack," Bellinger continued. "Assuming that he will not use more than twenty-seven knots for his run-in [to launch point], or launch from farther out than 200 miles, Catalinas taking off at dawn and flying 700 miles at 100 knots will guarantee effective coverage. With normal visibility of twenty-five miles, each Catalina can scan an 8° sector. It is desirable to scan 180° [the western semicircle], so twenty-three planes will be needed [180° divided by 8° = 22.5, or 23 planes]."

Admiral Nimitz supplied the planes.

An attack for the purpose of capturing Midway is expected. The attacking force may be composed of all combatant types including four or five carriers, transports, and train vessels. If presence of Task Forces 16 and 17 remains unknown to enemy we should be able to make surprise flank attacks on enemy carriers from position northeast of Midway. Further operations will be based on result of these attacks, damage inflicted by Midway forces, and information of enemy movements. The successful conclusion of the operation now commencing will be of great value to our country. Should carriers become separated during attacks by enemy aircraft, they will endeavor to remain within visual touch.

All that Nimitz could do now was stand and wait.

On the morning of June 3, Ensign Jewell H. "Jack" Reid piloted his Midway-based PBY Catalina flying boat on a course heading south-southwest. He did not know what to expect on that scouting patrol, but he felt as if something would happen soon.

"Stay very alert at your stations," he cautioned his crew. He later recalled proudly that they always had obeyed, willingly, even though "we had been flying over twelve hours per day for the past several days." That morning their efforts paid off.

At around 0900, Reid sighted a large number of transport vessels about seven hundred miles west of Midway. "My god, aren't those ships on the horizon?" he shouted to his copilot, Ensign Gerald Hardeman. "I believe we have hit the jackpot."

Ensign Jewell H. "Jack" Reid and his crew spotted what they believed to be the entire Japanese invasion force and immediately alerted U.S. aircraft carriers.

Reid had actually spotted the troop transports belonging to Admiral Kondo's Midway Invasion Force, but he thought them to be the main Japanese fleet. Reid radioed Midway at once: "Sighted Main Body." He sent a second message two minutes later: "Bearing 262 [degrees], distance 700 [miles]."

Midway received the messages, starting at 0925: The main Japanese fleet was seven hundred miles away and headed straight at Midway!

Far below, on the bridge of the escort flagship *Jintsu*, Rear Admiral Raizo Tanaka observed Reid's PBY overhead. The commander of the Transport Group (part of the Midway Invasion Force) immediately dispatched a message informing Yamamoto that all hopes for catching Midway by surprise were lost.

Fletcher Gambles

Admiral Fletcher on *Yorktown* learned of Reid's report right away. The veteran commander regarded the young ensign's analysis of the situation with serious misgivings, however. If Reid had truly sighted the main Japanese fleet, then Fletcher's task forces in the Point Luck area were not in a position to intercept it. But there had been no mention of carriers in Reid's report. Fletcher judged correctly that Reid had seen only elements of the invasion force. Gambling that the Japanese carrier attack would come out of the northwest commencing at dawn the next day, Fletcher elected to hold steady on course. Fletcher had made the correct decision, but he felt greatly relieved upon receipt of a coded message from Admiral Nimitz.

The message from CinCPAC, based on the latest intelligence reports, stated: "That is not repeat not the enemy striking force—stop—That is the landing force. The striking force will hit from the northwest at daylight tomorrow."

Fletcher corrected course to the southwest at 1950. The next morning found *Yorktown* in good position, some two hundred miles north and just east of Midway.

Within hours of Reid's sighting, nine Midway-based U.S. Army Air Corps B-17s, led by Lieutenant Colonel Walter Sweeney, located Admiral Tanaka's transports and unloaded thirty-six bombs on them. Several B-17 pilots claimed direct hits. Sweeney himself reported seeing a battleship and a transport remaining afloat "with huge clouds of dark smoke mushroomed above them." In truth, not one bomb had scored a hit on target.

Such inaccurate reporting was common. In fairness to the pilots, it should be pointed out that near misses often appeared as hits because they were viewed through flame and smoke and towering plumes of water. And amid the heat and flash of battle, reality glimpsed at varying angles and distances, under threat of death, often becomes distorted in the eyes of the observer.

Admiral Fletcher, commander of the USS Yorktown, *did not react to Jack Reid's message to attack the fleet he spotted.*

Admiral Nagumo's First Carrier Striking Force was to spearhead the attack at Midway.

"But Where Is the Enemy Fleet?"

Meanwhile, Admiral Nagumo's First Carrier Striking Force steamed blindly eastward through heavy seas, wrapped in low-hanging cloud cover and shifting fog. Navigating became extremely dangerous. The weather conditions prevented Nagumo from launching his observation aircraft, and Yamamoto insisted on keeping strict radio silence. Even though Tanaka, whose transports had been attacked by Sweeney's B-17s, had advised Yamamoto that the secret was out, Yamamoto refused to break radio silence himself to warn Nagumo in turn. So, Nagumo was forced to suffer the torment of commanding in a void.

Commander Fuchida observed his aging leader and wondered how much more stress Nagumo could stand and still perform efficiently. "I thought especially of the heavy burden of responsibility resting on the shoulders of . . . Admiral Nagumo, whose force was spearheading the attack," Fuchida wrote later. "Would he measure up to this responsibility?"

Nagumo's superiors had charged him with the destruction of the enemy fleet. "But where is the enemy fleet?" he kept asking his junior officers aboard *Akagi*. He neither expected nor received an answer.

Commence Launching

At 0245 on June 4, loudspeakers aboard *Akagi* sounded off, summoning pilots and crews to their aircraft. Nagumo looked on, still unaware of yesterday's B-17 attack on Tanaka's transports and confident of achieving surprise at Midway.

"The enemy is not yet aware of our plan," he told his staff, "and he has not yet detected our task force." He displayed signs of a growing confidence, adding, "There is no evidence of an enemy task force in our vicinity." Insofar as he knew.

Shortly after the loudspeakers sounded, operations officer Commander Minoru Genda left the ship's sick bay and joined Nagumo on *Akagi's* bridge. Genda, a brilliant young air officer who had planned much of the Pearl Harbor attack, had been suffering from pneumonia. Although still quite sick, Genda followed the roar of aircraft engines topside and reported to Nagumo. The admiral put his arm around Genda and asked how he felt.

Genda apologized for being absent for so long and said, "I have a slight temperature but am feeling much better now." The dull glint in his eyes revealed a man sicker than his words would indicate, but he was flushed with the excitement of battle.

Moments later, another sick-bay resident made his painful way to the bridge. Commander Mitsuo Fuchida, who had led the attack at Pearl Harbor and had been scheduled to spearhead the assault on Midway as well, refused to let an ulcer keep him below deck at such a historic moment. "I am not up to par," he told Genda. "But my pilots are in good shape. They didn't have much time for training, but they are ready and confident."

The appearance of both Genda and Fuchida provided an added boost to the already high morale and fighting spirit of *Akagi*'s officers and crew. They were then primed to strike a telling blow for their emperor and their homeland.

Steaming full into the wind, Nagumo's First Carrier Striking Force drew within 240 miles of Midway. On *Akagi*'s bridge, Nagumo checked the carrier's wind gauge for sufficient launch velocity. Then, satisfied, he commanded, "Commence launching."

It was 0430 on June 4, 1942.

Second Wave

Crew members cheered and waved caps as a Zero fighter streakēd across *Akagi*'s flight deck and lifted off into the surrounding blackness. Eight more Zeros and 18 dive-bombers quickly followed. Two miles off to port, *Hiryu* began launching aircraft, as *Soryu* and *Kaga* cleared their lighted decks of planes at the same time. In fifteen minutes, 108 aircraft circled about overhead, forming up. At precisely 0445, with Lieutenant Joichi Tomonaga leading the way in place of Fuchida, the first attack wave departed on a compass heading for Midway.

Fifteen minutes later, loudspeakers aboard *Akagi* blasted out new instructions: "Prepare second attack wave." And shortly before sunrise, the frantic activity on all four carriers started all over again.

With bells clanging and hearts racing, *Akagi*'s crew raised a second wave of aircraft from below decks. This time the flight deck of *Akagi* was lined with eighteen bombers armed with torpedoes, as was the deck of *Kaga*. The torpedoes anticipated a use against enemy ships rather than on ground installations, where such weapons would not be effective. The bombers aboard the smaller carriers *Hiryu* and *Soryu*, however, were loaded with bombs.

Waiting and Wondering

Less than an hour earlier, at 0415, eleven Catalinas had taken off from Midway to begin their morning patrol. Fifteen B-17 bombers followed the PBYs into the predawn skies, hoping to make contact with the Japanese force. A mixed bag of aircraft remained on Midway: four army Martin B-26 Marauders, their bellies sliced to carry torpedoes; six navy Grumman TBF Avengers, a new type of torpedo bomber on loan from Torpedo Squadron 8 off *Hornet*; and the fighters and bombers of Marine Aircraft Group 22, comprising nineteen sadly outdated Brewster F2A Buffaloes and six newer Grumman F4F Wildcats of fighter squadron

VMF-221, and a split collection of old Chance-Vought SB2U Vindicators and new Douglas SBD Dauntlesses belonging to scout bombing squadron VMSB-241.

All the aircraft had been manned since 0315. Pilots and crews then sat staring at the lightening skies, complaining grumpily about the long periods of "hurry up and wait." Can battle be any worse? As they sat and wondered, Tomonaga's first attack wave of Mitsubishi Zero fighters, Aichi D3A1 Val dive-bombers, and Nakajima B5N Kate torpedo bombers—thirty-six of each—was droning steadily toward them with an answer.

"Attack Enemy Carriers"

At 0435, Fletcher on *Yorktown* also sent out search planes. But the enemy carriers, still shrouded in fog and mist, remained undetected by ten Dauntlesses from Fletcher's flagship. The thrill of discovery went instead to lieutenants Howard Ady and William Chase of PBY Flight 58. Through a break in the shifting cloud cover, they sighted the feathery wake of one of Nagumo's ships. When Ady and Chase dropped down for a closer look at 0530, the entire *Kido Butai*—Carrier Striking Force—came into their view. They immediately radioed an all-too-brief alarm to Midway: "Enemy carriers."

Fletcher intercepted the message, but, to his frustration, it gave him more questions than answers. How many were there? Where were they? And where were they headed? He would have to wait to find out.

While Fletcher awaited more information, Ady and Chase circled around, darting in and out of covering clouds, trying to avoid Japanese antiaircraft fire and a fighter plane that had been sent after them. Then they spotted Tomonaga's attack directly below. Again they crackled off a radio message, this time with more details: Many planes heading Midway, bearing 320°, distance 150." Fletcher was already plotting Nagumo's position when a third message reported: "Two carriers and a battleship, bearing 320°, distance 180, course 135, speed 25."

Forced to await the return of his Dauntlesses, Fletcher ordered Spruance and Task Force 16 to "proceed southwesterly and attack enemy carriers when definitely located. I will follow as soon as planes recovered."

At 0500, Number Four reconnaissance plane was launched from the heavy cruiser *Tone*, flagship of Rear Admiral Hiroaki Abe. Abe commanded the Support Group assigned to Nagumo's First Carrier Striking Force. The launching of Number Four plane had been delayed for a half-hour, supposedly because of a faulty catapult. If it had been launched on time, Number Four plane would have flown over Task Force 16 six minutes before Spruance started to launch his aircraft.

(Right) Marines arrive at Midway Island. (Above) B-17 Flying Fortresses take off from Midway Island to intercept and bomb the Japanese fleet.

Oddly, when asked later about the launch delay, the *Tone's* communications officer could not recall a problem. "There was no fact that catapults [catapult-launched aircraft] and others [other aircraft] had troubles to delay their departures," he said. The issue remains unresolved to this day.

First Wave Arrives

At Midway, radar soon picked up the oncoming attack wave. All hands stood primed for action. Air raid sirens blared, antiaircraft guns cranked into position, troops scurried to fighting stations, and aircraft lifted skyward. The B-17s already in the air seeking the invasion force were diverted to strike at the carriers. The four Marauders and six Avengers, all carrying torpedoes, climbed out of Eastern Island's airstrip and angled off toward the carriers, along with Vindicator and Dauntless dive-bombers from VMSB-241.

At 0630 U.S. Marines commenced raising of morning colors at Midway just as Tomonaga's wave arrived. They completed the flag-raising ceremony without regard to "bombs bursting in air."

CHAPTER THREE

Nagumo's Decisions

"His [Admiral Nagumo's] force was well balanced and appeared greatly superior in strength. Therefore, it would be easy to destroy the enemy if all his striking power were thrown into a single massive attack. Such strategy was orthodox [standard], but it had one flaw—neglect of the time factor. Victory in battle does not always go to the stronger; it often goes to the side which is quicker to act boldly and decisively to meet unforeseen developments, and to grasp fleeting opportunities."

—Mitsuo Fuchida and Masatake Okumiya in Midway

Gallant but sadly overmatched Buffaloes and Wildcats of marine fighter squadron VMF-221 reached out to greet the bulk of Tomonaga's attack wave about thirty miles offshore. The marines had aptly nicknamed their Buffaloes "Flying Coffins." The Wildcats were newer and better but did not approach the quality and capabilities of the Zero. Thus did 25 aging American fighters, machines that time had long since ceased to favor, face off against 108 of the finest aircraft that Japan could put in the air. The results were all too predictable. The marines lost fifteen aircraft in the fray. Of their ten returning planes, only two remained operational. Six of Tomonaga's warbirds would not return to the nest.

Second Lieutenant Charles M. Kunz, one of the Buffalo pilots, knocked down a Japanese bomber but barely escaped death himself. A Zero on his tail sent bullets whizzing by each side of his head, creasing his scalp above each ear. Kunz landed safely,

The personnel of VMF-221 on return from the Battle of Midway. The group faced the Japanese in sadly outdated planes.

but his plane was so badly riddled that it could not be used again. He later expressed mild criticism of the aircraft: "As for the F2A-3, it should be in Miami as a training plane, rather than be used as a first line fighter." Marine Aircraft Group 22 commander Lieutenant Colonel Ira E. Kimes later recalled, "It was necessary for the group surgeon to give [Kunz] several 'stiff shots' that night in order to induce him to sleep."

Wildcat pilot Second Lieutenant Roy A. Corry Jr. shot down a Zero and a Val dive-bomber before scooting for home with a badly leaking fuel tank. He praised the Zero as "by far the most maneuverable plane that exists at the present time. You cannot compare them with our service type ships." He also pointed out that the Japanese machines were not without faults. "The Japanese planes seem to be very vulnerable if you are fortunate enough to bring your guns to bear." But that took some doing.

Midway Raid

The raid on Midway lasted twenty minutes. The Japanese enjoyed almost a free run of the atoll, dumping hundreds of bombs on both Sand and Eastern Islands. Barracks, buildings, fuel tanks, a seaplane hangar—all were destroyed or set ablaze. Thirteen Americans died in the attack; another eighteen suffered wounds.

The First Attack Wave

"Over-all commander of the first attack wave was Lieutenant Joichi Tomonaga," wrote Mitsuo Fuchida, "personally leading 36 Type-97 level bombers from *Soryu* and *Hiryu*. To his left followed 36 Type-99 dive bombers from *Akagi* and *Kaga*, led by Lieutenant Shoichi Ogawa, a *Kaga* squadron commander. Lieutenant Masaharu Suganami of *Soryu* led the fighter escort of 36 Zeros (nine from each carrier). One hundred and eight planes in all.

"This was Tomonaga's first sortie [attack flight] of the Pacific War," Fuchida went on. "He had reported to *Hiryu* just before her departure from the homeland. He was, however, a veteran of the Sino-Japanese war and a capable and experienced flier, well qualified to lead the attack. Lieutenant Ogawa, a gallant pilot, had been in every action of the Nagumo Force since Pearl Harbor. His skill and daring were unequalled in the Naval Air Corps. Lieutenant Suganami, like most of the pilots, was also a veteran of the Pacific war since the Pearl Harbor attack. Full of fighting spirit, he was a typical fighter pilot. All the other pilots were well trained, and most were experienced. They worked together well as a team."

Despite the heavy destruction inflicted by the first attack wave, the Japanese had expected more damaging results. Their disappointment was expressed by Fuchida and Okumiya:

> The absence of surprise sharply reduced the effectiveness of our attack. The fully alerted enemy had sent all of his planes aloft, some to intercept [head off] and attack, the others merely to take refuge. Finding no planes on the fields, Tomonaga's bombers attacked the hangars, which were easily destroyed, and the airstrip. But the loss of the empty hangars was of little significance, and it was next to impossible for so few planes to effectively damage the airstrip.

Interestingly, the Americans thought that the Japanese had left the runway on Eastern Island undamaged for their own future use.

Midway Island suffered extensive damage following the initial Japanese attack. At right, a bare infrastructure is all that remains of a burned-out hangar.

The main objective of the first Japanese air strike was to take out Midway's well-known offensive air capability. Before heading home, Tomonaga circled the atoll to assess the damage done by his pilots. Towers of black smoke attested to considerable destruction. But American antiaircraft guns continued to bang away in strength.

Tomonaga radioed a message to Admiral Nagumo on *Akagi*: "There is need for a second attack. Time: 0700."

Two Hares

Beyond the horizon on *Akagi*, Nagumo faced a dilemma. He knew that his position had been spotted earlier by Ady and Chase's PBY. That meant that American commanders had been informed by then of the presence of Japanese carriers in the area. Should he now mount a second attack against Midway? Or should he hold onto his aircraft and prepare for a possible attack from enemy carriers? To further muddle his choices, at that point he could only *assume* the presence of U.S. carriers.

Admiral Kusaka, Nagumo's chief of staff, recalled that the two choices suddenly made him feel "a little like a hunter chasing two hares at once." Although their mission was twofold—occupy Midway and destroy the American fleet—Yamamoto had emphasized that the destruction of the U.S. fleet was of prime importance. Both Kusaka and Nagumo would have been better prepared to cope with "two hares" if they had kept Yamamoto's priority uppermost in their minds.

As Kusaka discussed the choices with Admiral Nagumo and Commander Genda, the First Carrier Striking Force rushed on toward a location about 140 miles northwest of Midway. Nagumo expected to start recovering Tomonaga's planes there at about 0800. The force maintained battle positions, with the carriers steaming in a box formation—*Akagi* leading on the right, trailed by *Kaga*; *Hiryu* ahead on the left, *Soryu* behind. A protective screen of battleships, cruisers, and destroyers formed a large, loose ring around the boxed carriers. All crews stood at battle stations.

Americans Attack

Suddenly, at 0705, a leading destroyer hoisted a flag signaling "Enemy planes in sight!" The cruiser *Tone*'s main battery of guns opened fire. A bugler aboard *Akagi* blared the air raid alarm. *Agaki* reported "Nine enemy planes bearing 150 degrees, distance 25,000 meters [15 miles]" and headed straight for the planes at full-ahead speed. More urgent matters forced Nagumo to postpone his decision for the time being.

The four Marauders and six Avengers from Midway arrived on scene at 0708. *Akagi* opened fire. Nagumo sent up ten Zeros to engage the Americans at 0709. Lieutenant Langton Fieberling led his Torpedo 8 squadron mates to the attack, through a curtain of flak and three Zeros. Three of the Avengers took hits instantly, exploded, and cartwheeled into the water.

The Marauders, commanded by Captain James Collins, joined the attack, also trying to pass through an all-but-impassable wall of fire. Two Marauders were shot down; the second burst into flames right over *Akagi*'s bridge and plunged into the sea.

The intense defensive fire forced the Americans to release their "pickles" (torpedoes) from too far out. Such early releases enabled intended targets for the torpedoes to maneuver out of harm's way. Two B-26 Marauders and one TBF Avenger survived the torpedo run. Not one torpedo hit its target.

Still new to war, the Americans had a lot to learn. In its first combat assignment, the TBF Avenger served as a lesson in tactics, as a later report by Admiral Nimitz indicated: "Although the TBF is a well armed plane, it is obvious that it cannot go through fighter opposition without fighter protection." In war, most lessons are learned the hard way.

U.S. Avenger bombers like these dropped their load on the deck of Akagi *during the Battle of Midway. Avengers, due to their slow speed, needed fighter protection to survive in battle against the Japanese.*

First Decision

Although the land-based bombers were not able to inflict damage on Nagumo's *Kido Butai*, the torpedo attack convinced the Japanese commander of the need for a second attack on Midway. At 0715, Nagumo sent a message to each carrier: "Planes in second attack wave stand by to carry out attack today. Re-equip yourselves with bombs." It has been said that at that moment, Chuichi Nagumo made the most important decision of the Pacific war. Admiral Kusaka later recalled the circumstances that led to that decision.

> Nagumo and his staff well knew that Yamamoto's intention was to have at least one-half of the aircraft of the 1st [Carrier] Air Fleet prepared for attacks upon the expected enemy carrier force. In fact, they had been kept readied till the limit. Under the circumstances where enemy land-based planes commenced their attacks upon our force and the expected enemy carrier force would not be discovered, however, it was almost intolerable for a commander at the front to keep half its strength in readiness indefinitely only for an enemy force which might not be in the area after all.

Since no American ships had been reported and none were expected, Kusaka concluded that Nagumo's decision was "sound under the prevailing circumstances."

Second Decision

Hiryu and *Soryu* were unaffected by Nagumo's order in that their planes were already loaded for dive-bombing. But confusion ruled when *Akagi* picked up a message at 0728 from one of *Tone*'s search planes that had taken off late, possibly as a result of launcher problems. The scout reported sighting "10 ships, probably enemy" two hundred miles east of Nagumo. If the scout had taken off on time, the report would have been received a half-hour sooner, when Nagumo's bombers were still loaded with torpedoes and ready for use against carriers. As it happened, though, that latest report caught Nagumo's ordnance teams in the middle of their change-out from torpedoes to bombs. Nagumo halted the bomb switch temporarily at 0745. It was his second major decision.

Commander Genda recalled that the scout's message baffled *Akagi*'s bridge: "Nagumo and other staff officers felt we were thrown off our guard. At the same time, we were at a loss how to make an accurate judgment of the situation."

At 0747, Nagumo radioed a brisk message to *Tone*'s Number Four search plane: "Ascertain ship types and maintain contact."

Before Nagumo could make up his mind what to do next, his carrier force was set upon once again by land-based enemy aircraft: sixteen Dauntless and eleven Vindicator dive-bombers, plus fifteen B-17 heavy bombers from Midway.

Japanese Might Have Avoided Disaster

If the presence of American carriers had been detected earlier, the battle at Midway might have ended quite differently.

"Naturally enough," wrote Fuchida and Okumiya, "Nagumo was eager to devote maximum strength to the Midway attack and did not want to use any more planes for search than was absolutely necessary. Since he had no reason to suspect the presence of an enemy force in the area, he was satisfied that a single-phase search was adequate precaution against the unexpected."

The Japanese naval aviators continued their analysis of events by observing that "although poorly advised, a one-phase search despatched half an hour before sunrise might have been helpful if everything had worked out as planned. But the delay in launching *Tone*'s planes sowed a seed which bore fatal fruit for the Japanese in the ensuing naval action. Reviewing the full story of the battle on both sides, we now know that the enemy task force was missed by *Chikuma*'s search plane [assigned with *Tone*'s plane to cover the center search area] which, according to the plan, should have flown directly over it. The enemy force was discovered only when the belated *Tone* plane, on the line south of the *Chikuma* plane, was on the dog-leg of its search. Had Admiral Nagumo carried out an earlier and more carefully planned two-phased search . . . the disaster that followed might have been avoided."

Americans Attack Again

At 0748 squadron commander Major Lofton Henderson, of VMSB-241, led his marine pilots into a shallow-angle, glide-bombing approach against *Hiryu*. The glide-bombing method was far less effective than the navy's highly accurate, sharp-angle, "hell-diving" technique, which required more pilot skill. Henderson opted for the easier glide-bombing approach because only three of his pilots had logged any time in the new Dauntless SBDs. Defending Zeros proceeded to shoot half of Henderson's bombers out of the air. Henderson himself went down in flames. The eight remaining planes bored in on target and released all their bombs before breaking for home. The Dauntlesses lucky enough to make it back "were badly shot up and some were in very unflyable condition." The returning pilots reported seeing towering water spouts all around the twisting, turning carrier, but *Hiryu* managed to escape without a scratch.

Then Major Benjamin Morris's eleven older, slower Vindicator dive-bombers pursued the attack further. Out of position for runs at the carriers, the second batch of marines selected two battleships as targets. Two Vindicators went down during the action. A third Vindicator, homeward bound, splashed into the sea five miles from Midway. Morris's pilots claimed a hit on either *Haruna* or *Kirishima*. At best, they had scored only a near miss.

Navy SBDs attack a Japanese fleet off the shores of Midway. A successful strike left a Japanese ship burning (can be seen at center of photo).

Third Decision

At 0807, Admiral Nagumo finally heard some good news from *Tone*'s search plane. It reported that the ten enemy ships sighted earlier "are five cruisers and five destroyers." Staff intelligence officer Lieutenant Commander Kenjiro Ono felt elated.

"At last! Just as I thought," he said. "There are no carriers." But the chief of staff shook his head. "The message alone couldn't make it clear that no enemy carriers were there," Admiral Kusaka said later. "Nor could there be an enemy force without carriers in the reported area under the prevailing circumstances."

Even so, the tensions on *Akagi*'s bridge lessened, at least for the moment, and the commander continued to rearm his planes for a second strike against Midway. In effect, Admiral Nagumo's third key decision in the critical hours after daybreak was to cancel the order that had changed his first decision.

"For one thing," Kusaka explained, "I thought at the time that reversing the order of re-equipping attack planes with bombs at such a short interval would only result in adding up much confusion." Besides, the Japanese were still under attack.

At 0810 the B-17 Flying Fortresses arrived overhead, again under Colonel Sweeney's leadership, and dropped their bombs from twenty thousand feet. Nagumo's carriers turned and churned to avoid the bombs. The B-17s, at their high altitude, suffered no losses and returned safely to Midway. The U.S. pilots reported four hits on the carriers. But again, not one carrier had been touched.

High-altitude bombers such as the B-17 were ineffective against the Japanese carriers.

Shocking News

By 0820 the bombers were gone. For the fourth time that morning, the First Carrier Striking Force had beaten off an enemy attack. And for the fourth time it had escaped harm. But another threat arose immediately. *Tone's* Number Four plane reported: "Enemy force accompanied by what appears to be aircraft carrier bringing up rear." This news struck *Akagi's* bridge harder than all the errant bombs dropped that morning.

"I was indeed shocked," Admiral Kusaka recalled, "although such an eventuality was not entirely outside our consideration." Despite the stunning news, Kusaka saw no signs of panic or indecision in Nagumo's manner. "He might have been shocked for a moment," Kusaka continued, "but I think anyone facing such an unexpected eventuality would have been shocked for a moment."

Nagumo then faced a fourth vital decision. The fighter planes that had just defended his ships were still circling the carrier and were running low on fuel. They would have to come down for refueling before they could be used to escort Japanese bombers on a strike against enemy carriers.

To muddle the mix further, Tomonaga's first attack wave planes started arriving overhead at 0830, their fuel gauge needles shivering on the empty mark. They too had to be brought down before they ran out of fuel and crashed into the sea.

At this point, Rear Admiral Tamon Yamaguchi, commander of Carrier Division 2 (part of First Carrier Striking Force) aboard *Hiryu*, signaled a message to Nagumo: "Consider it advisable to launch attack force immediately." Yamaguchi, an impatient sort, held no great love for Nagumo and felt that he himself was better qualified to command the strike force. Nagumo, the admiral who had commanded the emperor's victorious forces at Pearl Harbor, disagreed in principle with Yamaguchi's recommendation to send unescorted bombers against enemy carriers that were sure to be heavily defended by fighters. An honest disagreement, but one that Nagumo would later regret.

Fourth Decision

Nagumo knew the importance of surprise and attacking swiftly with great force. But at that moment Nagumo had only thirty-six dive-bombers of *Hiryu* and *Soryu*, and a handful of torpedo bombers reequipped with bombs, available for launching. And every one of his fighter planes was in the air, running on empty. Nagumo would not commit his bombers

Rear Admiral Tamon Yamaguchi, commander of Carrier Division 2, believed that he was more qualified than Nagumo to command the strike force at Midway.

without fighter protection. Kusaka agreed.

"I was not entirely against [Yamaguchi's] view of launching the attack force without re-equipping," he said, "but I couldn't agree with him on the point of letting them go without fighter cover, because I witnessed how enemy planes without fighter cover were almost [wiped out] by our fighters [without mercy]. I wanted most earnestly to provide them with fighters by all means." But first the fighters must be fueled.

Commander Genda said, "It was a problem of whether more than one hundred crack planes of the first wave would be wasted in ditching in the sea or not." As air operations officer of the First Air Fleet, Genda knew that the loss of so many valuable pilots and crews would strike a severe blow to Japan's offensive capability. He agreed with Kusaka that "the previous engagement well showed that an attack force without fighter cover could inflict damage to an enemy force well protected by fighters." Genda thus advised Nagumo and Kusaka to delay launching an attack until all first-wave fighters were recovered.

To recover all his aircraft would cost Nagumo at least a half-hour. If American carriers were nearby, and Nagumo was by then convinced that they were, a thirty-minute delay could mean the difference between victory and defeat—not to mention life and death. Nagumo found himself torn between the urgency for mounting a swift attack on the reported American fleet on the one hand, and loyalty to his airmen on the other.

Nagumo decided immediately to bring in his fighters and rearm the bombers with torpedoes. Genda later stressed that "decisions were never delayed by indecision." Nagumo's fourth critical decision on the morning of June 4 would cost him and *Kido Butai* dearly.

Lieutenant Commander Minoru Genda drafted the first detailed plans of the attack on Pearl Harbor.

Quick Changes

Two minutes after receiving news of an enemy carrier, Nagumo flashed a message to his fleet: "Carrier based bombers will prepare for second attack. Equip yourselves with 250 kilogram bombs [550 pound torpedoes]."

Good-natured Shogo Masuda, air officer on *Akagi*, commented, "Here we go again! This is getting to be a quick-change contest." Some less-than-amused crew members, those who had to do the work, asked one another, "What the hell is Headquarters doing?"

At the same time, the order was given on each carrier to "Clear the deck to recover planes!" Followed at 0837 by raised signal flags that indicated "Commence landing!" The first plane touched down at 0838.

At 0918—*forty* minutes later—the last plane was recovered. Nagumo shifted course 90° to the east and increased speed to thirty knots. *Kido Butai* closed rapidly with U.S. Task Forces 16 and 17, which lay over the horizon. Crews worked at fever pitch on all four of Nagumo's carriers, preparing thirty-six dive-bombers, fifty-four torpedo bombers, and their fighter escorts for the coming encounter. Admiral Isoroku Yamamoto's long-awaited battle for control of the Pacific was set to begin.

In the bustle of recovering aircraft, a final message from *Tone*'s Number Four plane, oddly, went unnoticed aboard *Akagi*—or at least unacted upon. The message said: "Ten enemy torpedo planes are heading toward you."

CHAPTER FOUR

"To Sink the Enemy"

> "'Wise after the event,' the saying goes. Still there is no question that it would have been wiser to launch our dive bombers immediately, even without fighter protection. In such all-or-nothing carrier warfare, no other choice was admissible. Even the risk of sending unprotected level bombers should have been accepted as necessary in this emergency. Their fate would have probably have been the same as that of the unescorted American planes which had attacked us a short while before, but just possibly they might have saved us from the catastrophe we were about to suffer."
> —*Air Unit Commander Mitsuo I. Fuchida*

When Rear Admiral Frank Jack Fletcher received Ady and Chase's report of Nagumo's presence at 0530, both task forces under his overall command lay beyond striking distance of the enemy. Spruance's Task Force 16 was nearer, however, and in a quick, unselfish action, Admiral Fletcher ordered Spruance to "attack enemy carriers when definitely located," effectively handing battle command responsibility to his brother officer. Fletcher had not hesitated to shift his command to where it rightfully belonged: with the field commander who was closer to the action. He had placed the command in good hands.

Spruance Takes Command

Rear Admiral Raymond A. Spruance was a bright, thoughtful man, known to take chances only when the reward equaled the risk. At the same time, his strong will and aggressive fighting

spirit made him an ideal choice to lead the hunt for Nagumo's flattops (carriers). Spruance looked forward to their destruction.

"That was my mission: to get those Japanese carriers and then protect and preserve Midway from the enemy," he recalled. At the outset, he made two important decisions that would ultimately determine the battle's outcome.

Spruance's original approach to the impending action favored holding off his strike until Task Force 16 drew within a hundred miles of Nagumo's carrier force. That would have meant launching his aircraft at approximately 0900. It also would have allowed his pilots a margin for error in which to find the enemy, attack, and return. But word about the Japanese attack on Midway prompted Captain Miles Browning, Spruance's chief of staff, to recommend an immediate strike.

Naval historian Samuel E. Morison described Browning as "one of the most irascible [cranky] and unstable officers ever to earn a fourth stripe, but a man with a slide-rule brain." Browning was an air officer who knew his business well. Browning figured that the Japanese would try to launch a second attack against Midway. Why not try to catch Nagumo in the act of refueling his planes?

The greater distance entailed by opting for an immediate launch increased the risk tenfold, adding an equal measure of pain to Spruance's decision. Browning estimated Nagumo's position to be about 155 miles away, thus almost eliminating any safety margin. This raised the probability that more than a few American planes would run out of fuel and splash into the ocean. Spruance well knew, however, that a good commander must stand ready to risk the lives of a few so that the many may survive. Spruance also knew the overriding importance of maintaining surprise and striking hard before the enemy discovers the attackers.

One of Rear Admiral Raymond A. Spruance's strengths as a commanding officer was his ability to take suggestions from those under him, such as Captain Miles Browning (bottom).

"Launch Everything You Have"

Spruance was not above acting on the advice of a junior officer, and to his great credit, he elected to launch right away. To his further credit, Spruance decided to commit every available aircraft—holding back only observation planes—to the destruction of Nagumo's *Kido Butai.*

"Launch everything you have at the earliest possible moment and strike the enemy carriers," Spruance said to Browning on the bridge of *Enterprise*. "I figured that if I were going to hit the Japanese," Spruance recalled later, "I should hit them with everything I had." He figured right.

At about 0700, *Enterprise* and *Hornet* turned into the wind and commenced launching.

Among the first to lift off *Hornet*'s flight deck was the main body of Lieutenant Commander John C. Waldron's Torpedo (squadron) 8 (VT-8), consisting of fifteen ancient Douglas Devastators. Waldron, a navy career pilot from South Dakota, square-jawed and proud of his Sioux Indian heritage, was liked and admired by superiors and juniors alike.

In a letter to his wife the night before the battle, Waldron had written, "If I do not come back—well, you and the little girls can know that this squadron struck for the highest objective in naval warfare—'To sink the enemy.'"

Then, to conclude a last message to his men on the eve of battle, he wrote: "If there is only one plane left to make a final run in, I want that man to go in and get a hit. May God be with all of us. Good luck, happy landings, and give 'em hell!"

A B-25 bomber launches off the USS Hornet *to take part in air raids over Japan.*

Besides Torpedo 8, *Hornet* launched 35 Dauntless dive-bombers (VB-8 and VS-8) and 10 Wildcat fighters (VF-8), a total (including Waldron's Devastators) of 60 aircraft, all under Commander Stanhope C. Ring, the leader of the carrier's Air Group 8.

Off *Enterprise's* heaving flight deck rose a near match to *Hornet's* swarm: 10 Wildcats (VF-6), 33 Dauntlesses (VB-6 and VS-6), and 14 Devastators (VT-6)—the entire complement of Air Group 6, under Lieutenant Commander Clarence W. McClusky Jr.

Launch operations concluded at 0806. One hundred seventeen planes of Spruance's Task Force 16 formed up overhead and roared off over the southwest horizon toward their targets, now approximately 150 miles away. *Enterprise* and *Hornet* turned back out of the wind and followed.

Fletcher's *Yorktown*, sailing some fifteen miles behind Spruance to the east, completed the launch of half its aircraft an hour later at 0906. Thus 17 Dauntlesses (VB-3), 12 Devastators (VT-3), and 6 Wildcats (VF-3) also took up the hunt for *Kido Butai*.

A plane takes off from the USS Yorktown *during the Battle of* Midway.

Two Turns

Twelve minutes later, Nagumo executed his 90° turn in the general direction of the U.S. fleet. Nagumo knew that his new course of north-northeast would help him to avoid further attacks by Midway-based planes. What he did not know was that his change of course also turned him away from 152 American carrier planes trying to find him. Nagumo's luck had not entirely deserted him.

Shortly after Nagumo changed course, the dive-bombers and fighters from *Hornet* arrived at the point calculated to put them in contact with the Japanese carriers. Commander Stanhope Ring had planned a coordinated attack of dive-bombers and torpedo bombers. But his Dauntlesses had become separated from Waldron's Devastators while forming up. Now, on station, Ring saw only clouds to his right and open sea and sky elsewhere. No *Kido Butai*. No Waldron. Nothing. Actually, *Kido Butai* lay hidden beneath the covering clouds. Ring, however, guessing that Nagumo had headed toward Midway, slanted off in that direction—away from the Japanese admiral's flattops.

Torpedo Squadron 8

Jack Waldron's Torpedo 8 reached the designated map location right after Ring's group had flown off toward Midway. Instead of following Ring, however, Waldron played a hunch and veered north.

Ensign George H. Gay, a VT-8 pilot, recalled later that Waldron had informed his pilots earlier "not to worry about their navigation; just follow him, for he knew where he was going." And that he did, as Gay further recalled: "We went just as straight to the Jap Fleet as if he'd had a string tied to them."

What inner sense guided Waldron that day will never be known, but his hunch paid off. Seemingly on cue, the clouds parted and suddenly there, eight miles off Waldron's starboard wing and far below, lay *Kido Butai*.

The creaking Devastators of Torpedo 8, having lost contact with their contingent of Wildcats, commenced their attempts "to sink the enemy" at 0920, without benefit of fighter protection. With Waldron in front, they dropped down to wave-top height and began their runs, each pilot picking the closest carrier for a target. Set upon at once from above by a swarm of some thirty Zeros, and met by a wall of exploding steel, they flew without pause into the face of death. Waldron led the way, and the VT-8 pilots followed their revered leader with perfect trust and loyalty.

"We could almost look at the back of Commander Waldron's head and know what he was thinking," Ensign Gay said later, "because he had told us so many times over and over just what we should do under all conditions."

Ensign George Gay (left) was the only man to survive his torpedo squadron's attack on Japanese carriers. Gay was shot out of the sky during the attack, which suffered high losses because the bombers did not have fighter protection. Gay is seen here with Lt. E.S. McCuskey. The Japanese flags symbolize McCuskey's victories.

History has recorded little to reveal what happened in those final few minutes, when the members of Torpedo 8 gave their last full measure of devotion to their leader and their country. Waldron's voice was heard briefly over the radio in crackling, stunted bursts: "Watch those fighters! . . . Attack immediately! . . . See that splash! . . . How am I doing, Dobbs? [Radioman Horace Dobbs] . . . I'd give a million to know who did that. . . . There's two fighters in the water. . . . My two wing men are going in the water." Then Waldron went in.

The Last Man

Gay saw his commander's plane explode in flames from the left fuel tank. Waldron stood up and struggled to free himself from the flaming cockpit. Gay lost sight of him and never saw him again. The young ensign suddenly realized that his Devastator was the only American plane still flying. Recalling what Waldron had said about "only one plane left," Gay reported that he "flew right down the gun barrel of one of those big pom poms up forward [antiaircraft gun aboard his targeted carrier]."

Gay released his torpedo aimed at *Soryu*, but the carrier swerved sharply and the "pickle" sped by harmlessly. Not a single VT-8 torpedo found its target.

At 0940, Ensign George H. Gay, by then wounded, afloat in the embattled waters, was the only member of Torpedo 8 left alive. He clung to wreckage from his aircraft, keeping low in the water, and watched the unfolding battle. He was picked up the next day by a navy PBY searching for survivors.

A doctor asked Gay later how he had treated his wounds. Gay replied that he had soaked them "in salt water for several hours."

Just as an elated Zero flight leader was reporting to Nagumo that all fifteen torpedo bombers of VT-8 had been sent crashing into the sea in flames, a lookout aboard *Akagi* shouted: "Enemy torpedo bombers, thirty degrees to starboard, coming in low!"

Almost as an echo, a second lookout yelled: "Enemy torpedo bombers approaching forty degrees to port!"

Torpedo Squadrons 3 and 6

The torpedo planes of *Enterprise* and *Yorktown* had arrived over target at the same time. Fourteen Devastators of Torpedo 6 off *Enterprise*, led by Lieutenant Commander Eugene E. Lindsey, dove to the attack, also without benefit of fighter protection. Lindsey's VT-6 had been flying under the cloud cover at about fifteen hundred feet and experienced no difficulty in finding *Kido Butai*.

Unknown to Lindsey (and Waldron before him), Lieutenant James S. Gray's ten Wildcats of Fighting 6 (VF-6) off *Enterprise* were also over target, circling unseen above the cloud cover at twenty thousand feet. Lindsey had agreed before the mission to call Gray for help if Torpedo 6 ran into trouble. But since Lindsey never sighted VF-6 above the cloud cover, he did not request help by radioing the agreed-upon appeal: "Come on down, Jim." Gray's fighters eventually headed home without engaging the enemy.

A damaged Avenger torpedo plane is the sole survivor of the Torpedo 6 squadron which initially boasted eight Avengers.

Ten of Lindsey's Devastators, including his own, were shot to pieces by antiaircraft fire and a throng of Zeros; they went tumbling aflame into the sea. The four surviving planes released their torpedoes without hitting their elusive targets.

Diving next in a shrieking attack came Lieutenant Commander Lance E. "Lem" Massey's Torpedo 3 (VT-3) Devastators off *Yorktown*, in company with six Wildcats. The Wildcats belonged to *Yorktown*'s Fighting 3 (VF-3) and were commanded by Lieutenant Commander John S. "Jimmy" Thach. Outnumbered two to one by the swarming Zeros, three of the Wildcats fell to enemy guns and splashed into the ocean. A few Zeros kept the three remaining Wildcats busy, while most of the Japanese fighters turned their attention to Massey's Devastators.

(Top) The Devastators of Torpedo 6 aboard USS Enterprise *prepare for takeoff. Only four planes of this squadron returned after engaging the enemy. (Right) A Grumman Wildcat takes off from the USS* Yorktown *during the Battle of Midway.*

The Thach Weave

The U.S. Navy's F4F Wildcat came in second in a two-plane race when matched against the Zero. This, of course, represented a real problem for the Americans. The answer lay in tactics. Lieutenant Commander John S. "Jimmy" Thach, commander of *Yorktown*'s fighter squadron VF-5, came up with the solution.

"Fight as a team and you'll live longer," Thach told his pilots in early 1942. He then proceeded to instruct them in the aerial maneuver that still bears his name: the "Thach weave."

The tactic called for the use of a four-plane formation composed of two sections, rather than the traditional three-plane element. Having the fourth aircraft enabled the planes to fight in pairs. Two planes would fly a parallel route until attacked. When a Zero locked on a Wildcat's tail, the paired Wildcats would bank sharply inward.

"The quick turn toward each other does two things to the enemy pilot," Thach explained. "It throws off his aim and, because he usually tries to follow his target, it leads him around into a position to be shot by the other member of our team."

The "Thach weave" worked so well that the navy adopted it as standard practice, as did also the U.S. Army Air Cops, the British Royal Air Force, and the Soviet air force.

Lieutenant Commander Jimmy Thach was considered an exceptional aerial gunner. The Japanese flags indicate the number of Japanese fighters Thach shot down.

By then, Massey himself had closed to within a mile of *Akagi*. As he turned to commence his torpedo run, a Zero shot him down in flames. Six of his squadron mates met a similar fate. The five Devastators that were left managed to get off their torpedoes, but not one found its mark. Then three of the remaining five Devastators crashed into the sea in flames. The last two returned home intact.

By 1000 on the morning of June 4, thirty-five of forty-one American torpedo bombers sent to attack *Kido Butai* had been shot down. Sixty-nine of eighty-five pilots and crew members rode to their deaths in Devastators, including three squadron commanders. Nine torpedoes were released on target, but not a single one found its mark.

When measured against damage inflicted on the enemy, the sacrifices of the American torpedo squadrons might seem to have been made for nothing. Not so. Their deaths bought time; time in which Japanese launch preparations were delayed—*time that enabled one last chance for an American victory at Midway*.

All that remained by then of the American strike force were the dive-bombers, and they still could not find Nagumo's carriers.

Of Commander Ring's thirty-five Dauntlesses, twenty-two used their last drops of fuel returning to *Hornet*. Thirteen remaining Dauntlesses and ten Wildcats continued an unsuccessful search for *Kido Butai*, then attempted to reach Midway. Ten Dauntlesses made it safely to the atoll on fumes. The Wildcats and the remaining bombers splashed into the ocean. Rescuers from Midway picked up eight pilots. The rest perished.

While Ring's Air Group 8 searched unsuccessfully for *Kido Butai* in the direction of Midway, Lieutenant Commander Maxwell Leslie's seventeen Dauntlesses searched the ocean southeast of the Japanese carriers with a similar lack of success.

McClusky's Decision

Meanwhile, Lieutenant Commander Clarence McClusky, leading the Dauntlesses of VB-6 and VS-6 off *Enterprise*, had also failed to find *Kido Butai*. His group then numbered thirty-one, since two Dauntlesses had been lost to engine trouble along the way. As instructed, he had led them on a bearing of 240° over a span of 155 miles. So far, he had seen no trace of the enemy.

McClusky then faced a critical decision: Should he continue on course or change direction? Either he had beaten *Kido Butai* to the target area or Nagumo's carriers had already passed the spot on their way to Midway. He could see miles of open sea to his left and felt pretty sure that the Japanese carrier force had not passed. That told McClusky that he could either keep going or turn right. In either case, he was within fifteen minutes of reaching the point of no return and had to decide quickly. He looked at his map and decided to continue on a bearing of 240° for fifteen minutes, then turn right. The gods of battle upheld his decision.

Captain George D. Murray, commanding officer of *Enterprise*, called McClusky's decision "the most important decision of the entire action." Admiral Nimitz later seconded the opinion, declaring that McClusky's decision was "one of the most important decisions of the battle and one that had decisive results."

At 0948, McClusky turned right and started flying northwest, hoping that the new course would put him on a line with Nagumo's southbound carriers. About seven minutes later, McClusky spotted the white wake of a Japanese destroyer. It had left *Kido Butai* to chase off the American submarine *Nautilus*, which had been threatening the Japanese force. McClusky

Lieutenant Commander Clarence McClusky's daring actions during the Battle of Midway allowed U.S. bombers to locate the Japanese aircraft carriers.

followed the destroyer, in the belief that it would lead him to the carriers.

Over his radio at about the same time, he heard the voice of Captain Browning, excitedly urging, "Attack! Attack!"

"Wilco!" McClusky snapped, "as soon as I find the bastards!" He maintained course for another anxious twenty minutes, his fuel gauge by then starting to dip below the halfway mark. At 1020, stretching the limits of safe return, McClusky finally found Nagumo's First Carrier Striking Force. He shot off another brief message to *Enterprise*: "I've found the Jap."

McClusky first ordered VB-6 squadron leader Lieutenant Richard H. Best, flying a little below and behind him, to attack the carrier farthest to the right. It was *Akagi*. Then, to the VS-6 squadron leader Lieutenant W. Earl Gallaher, flying beside him, McClusky said, "Earl, you follow me down." McClusky had selected *Kaga*, the nearer carrier, as the second target.

By chance, Commander Leslie's seventeen Dauntlesses arrived over *Kido Butai* at the same time. Leslie spotted *Hiryu* and *Soryu* through a break in the clouds and signaled his pilots to attack. The time was 1024. Then the sky fell on *Kido Butai*.

"Six Minutes That Changed the World"

About twenty thousand feet below the American dive-bombers, the Japanese carriers had just swung around into the wind. Aircraft lined the flight decks of all four carriers. Engines roared in final warm-up. Pilots awaited the flags that would launch Nagumo's first strike against the American carriers.

At exactly 1024, the first Zero escort rolled down *Akagi*'s flight deck and took to the air. Commander Mitsuo Fuchida remembered watching the Zero lift off and feeling relieved, until "at that instant a lookout screamed: 'Dive bomber!'"

Fuchida gazed skyward at the lookout's warning and saw "three black enemy planes plummeting toward our ship. The plump silhouette of the American Dauntless dive-bombers quickly grew larger, and then a number of black objects suddenly floated eerily from their wings. Bombs! Down they came straight toward me!"

Somehow, Lieutenant Best had not received the word from McClusky to attack the carrier farthest away. Thus Best assumed that his group, as the trailing group, would take the nearer carrier. This was standard practice. As a result of the confusion, most of VB-6's Dauntlesses joined VS-6's attack on *Kaga*. But the rest, five in all, screamed down on *Akagi*.

Japanese carriers Kaga *and* Akagi *under attack by U.S. dive-bombers.*

Four bombs struck *Kaga* in quick succession. Three more bombs hit *Akagi*, setting off multiple bomb and torpedo explosions among *Akagi's* aircraft. Fire from ruptured fuel tanks flared up and fanned out above and below decks. As the fires spread, *Akagi* became, in Admiral Kusaka's words, "a burning hell." Only minutes later, Kusaka urged Admiral Nagumo to transfer his flag elsewhere.

"But Nagumo, having a feeling heart, refused to listen to me," Kusaka recalled. "I urged him two or three times, but in vain. He firmly continued to stand by the side of the compass on the bridge."

Then Captain Aoki, an old classmate of Nagumo's from Eta Jima, the imperial naval academy, approached and spoke to Nagumo softly: "Chief of Staff, as the ship's captain I am going to take care of this ship with all responsibility, so I urge you, the Commander in Chief, and all other staff officers to leave this vessel as soon as possible, so that the command of the force may be continued."

Nagumo finally gave in and transferred his command to the light cruiser *Nagara*. Commander Fuchida was the last officer to leave *Akagi*, scrambling down a rope that was already burning.

Meanwhile, at 1025, Maxwell Leslie led VB-3 in a dive on *Soryu*, but his guns jammed while firing on *Soryu's* bridge on the way down. Leslie swerved from the attack and "retired for four-and-a-half minutes at high speed to the SE. . . ." Lieutenant (j.g.) Paul A. "Lefty" Holmberg took over the lead of VB-3.

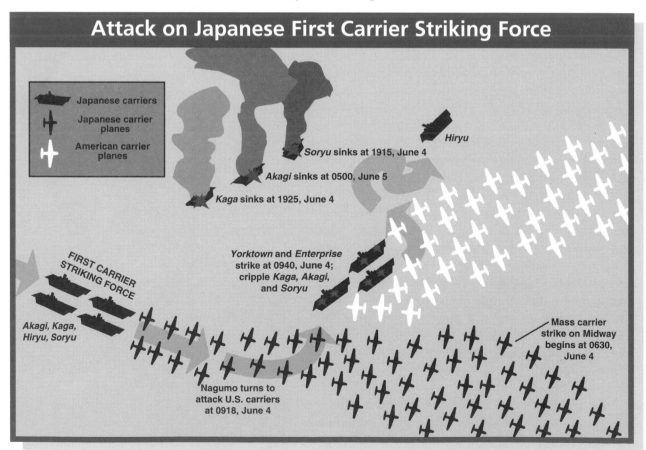

Attack on Japanese First Carrier Striking Force

Japanese carriers

Japanese carrier planes

American carrier planes

Hiryu

Soryu sinks at 1915, June 4

Akagi sinks at 0500, June 5

Kaga sinks at 1925, June 4

FIRST CARRIER STRIKING FORCE

Yorktown and *Enterprise* strike at 0940, June 4; cripple *Kaga*, *Akagi*, and *Soryu*

Akagi, Kaga, Hiryu, Soryu

Mass carrier strike on Midway begins at 0630, June 4

Nagumo turns to attack U.S. carriers at 0918, June 4

The flight deck crew aboard the USS Yorktown *rushes to secure Douglas Dauntlesses that have just returned from a strike on Japanese forces.*

"Five direct hits and three very near misses were scored immediately thereafter," as Third Division leader Lieutenant D.W. Shumway later described the action.

Fierce deck fires broke out immediately on *Soryu*, triggering explosions in bomb, torpedo, and ammunition storage rooms, and in fuel tanks. Of the three carriers struck so far, *Soryu* suffered the most immediate and severe damage. Within twenty minutes, it lay hopelessly engulfed in flames. Ten minutes later, Captain Ryusaku Yanagimoto, *Soryu*'s commander, ordered, "Abandon ship!" As the crew obeyed, Yanagimoto stood on the signal tower to the right of *Soryu*'s bridge and shouted, "*Banzai!*"

A chief petty officer named Abe climbed to the tower, saluted his captain, and said, "Captain, I have come on behalf of all your men to take you to safety. They are waiting for you. Please come with me to the destroyer, sir." Abe, a former wrestling champion, moved forward to pick up and carry his captain to safety.

Yanagimoto stared at Abe, then turned his back to him without saying a word. Abe saluted again and left. As Abe moved off the tower, tears streaming down his cheeks, he could hear Yanagimoto softly singing "Kimigayo," the Japanese national anthem. The captain went down with his ship.

In a six-minute attack—Samuel Morison's "six minutes that changed the world"—fifty-two American dive-bombers had destroyed three of *Kido Butai*'s four carriers. The next daybreak would find all three—*Kaga*, *Akagi*, and *Soryu*—resting forever at the bottom of the sea. Only *Hiryu* remained. But not for long.

All Honor to All Who Took Part

Historian Gordon W. Prange suggests three main factors for the success of the dive-bomber attacks after all earlier attacks that morning had failed: "McClusky's decision to continue his search with an unconventional pattern, the uncoordinated coordination which brought the *Enterprise* and *Yorktown* pilots on the spot within seconds of each other, and the preoccupation of the Zeros with the torpedo attacks."

Amazingly, all *Yorktown*'s aircraft made it home. The *Enterprise* group was less fortunate, losing fourteen aircraft, some of which ran out of fuel and splashed down.

The dive-bombers had struck at their targets almost without opposition. An overhead blanket of Zeros had been brought down to just off the water by the earlier attacks by torpedo bombers. And the same torpedo-bomber attacks on Nagumo's carriers had delayed the critical rearming of *Kido Butai*'s bombers. Consequently, three of the Japanese carriers never launched their aircraft in an intended attack that might have proved fatal to Fletcher's task forces.

America honors the accomplishments of its dive-bomber pilots in the Battle of Midway, and most deservedly so. But America cannot measure less the contributions of its torpedo-bomber pilots who tried so mightily "to sink the enemy."

CHAPTER FIVE

Deadly Duel

". . . command of air operations passed to Rear Admiral Tamon Yamaguchi, Commander Carrier Division 2 [part of First Carrier Striking Force], whose flagship, Hiryu, *was the only carrier left undamaged after the devastating enemy attack. . . . With no time to lose, Rear Admiral Yamaguchi immediately decided to launch an attack on the American carriers. The attack force, consisting of 18 dive bombers and 6 escorting Zero fighters, took off at 1040. It was commanded by Lieutenant Michio Kobayashi, who had been with the Nagumo Force in every campaign."*
—*Mitsuo Fuchida and Masatake Okumiya in* Midway

Lt. Michio Kobayashi led the attack on the USS Yorktown *during the Battle of Midway.*

At 1040, while the battle still raged around it, *Hiryu* managed to launch eighteen dive-bombers and six fighters. They represented the last chance for Admiral Isoroku Yamamoto's Combined Fleet to turn a stunning defeat into a glorious victory. If Japan were to prevail at Midway, the *Hiryu* attack force, led by Lieutenant Michio Kobayashi, could not fail in its mission to find and destroy the American carriers.

Fate stepped in immediately to play an odd role in helping Kobayashi and his pilots find *Yorktown*. They simply tagged along behind Maxwell Leslie's dive-bombers, as the VB-3 Dauntlesses winged their way home. The Americans unknowingly led the Japanese planes directly to Admiral Fletcher's flagship. It is unlikely that the Japanese could have found *Yorktown* by themselves.

Patience Under Pressure

"On *Enterprise*, Spruance and his staff studied the implications of the attack on *Yorktown* and what to do about it," wrote historian Gordon W. Prange. "Browning came to the obvious and correct conclusion that the planes striking the carrier originated from the undamaged Japanese flattop McClusky's pilots had reported. [They had reported sighting a fourth carrier upon returning from their attack on Nagumo's other three carriers.] The peppery chief of staff urged an immediate retaliation. Spruance refused to go off half-cocked. In the first place, his bombers were not yet ready for takeoff. In the second, he wanted a definite position report on the enemy carrier from scouts at that very minute approaching the anticipated location. Inability to find the enemy had already dissipated quite enough American strength for one battle.

"Yamaguchi [Carrier Division 2 commander aboard *Hiryu*] would have despised Spruance's caution, but once more the American admiral had made the right decision. . . . In all probability, an American attack at that time would have missed the carrier altogether, and could not have saved *Yorktown*."

First Attack on *Yorktown*

Leslie's planes found *Yorktown* just where it was supposed to be at about noon. They attempted to land but were promptly waved off and ordered out of antiaircraft zones. Radar had picked up a flight of unidentified aircraft forty-six miles out and closing fast. The ship's loudspeaker blared: "Stand by to repel enemy air attack! All hands lie down on deck. Air department take cover. Gunnery department take over."

Twelve *Yorktown* Wildcats patrolling overhead immediately tore into the Val bombers and Zero fighters of Kobayashi's attack wave. Down below, Captain Elliot Buckmaster, *Yorktown*'s skipper, swung his ship around in an evasive action. Antiaircraft gunners began banging away at the approaching aircraft.

Gun crews man their stations aboard the USS Yorktown.

An epic air encounter commenced, matching superior Zeros against more numerous Wildcats, twisting and tumbling and battling across the sky toward *Yorktown*. Lieutenant William Barnes pounced on the lead Val at about 12,000 feet. "I came in on him on a high side run. My guns were wide open and ripping into him. He went down smoking." Barnes dispatched a second Val in like fashion "boring down on him from the side and shooting him to pieces." He nailed a third bomber before "three Zeros got on my tail and it was nip and tuck as I worked down to 9,000 feet and then dove off through a big cloud layer for about 2,000 feet to shake them off." Barnes made it safely to *Hornet*, but his Wildcat was riddled with holes.

While Admiral Fletcher hunched over a chart on *Yorktown*'s bridge, one of his staff officers entered and informed him, "The attack is coming in, sir."

"Well, I've got on my tin hat," Fletcher replied pleasantly. "I can't do anything else now."

Seven of Kobayashi's dive-bombers broke through the ring of defending Wildcats. Of those seven, three scored direct hits on *Yorktown*, which still bore great scars from the Coral Sea contest. One bomb pierced the carrier's side and knocked out two of its boilers. The other two bombs set off roaring blazes. A rag stowage compartment erupted in flames, sending off billowing clouds of black smoke. By 1230, *Yorktown* stood dead in the water.

The seven Vals that had dived paid dearly for their hits, all seven of them, including Kobayashi's, falling to American guns. Only five of eighteen Vals and three of six Zeros made it back to *Hiryu*.

Yorktown's wounds, though severe, were not terminal. Repair crews set to work right away to fix the damage. Admiral Fletcher could not wait, however, and transferred his flag to the cruiser *Astoria*. He still had a fleet to run, and a disabled carrier was not the best place from which to run it.

Second Attack on *Yorktown*

Nor were the *Yorktown*'s troubles over yet. Earlier, Admiral Yamaguchi, temporarily in command of *Kido Butai*, learned the true size of the American fleet for the first time. Upon sighting the vessels at about 1140, Kobayashi's attack unit had radioed *Hiryu*: "Enemy air force has as its nucleus three carriers. These are accompanied by 22 destroyers." (The observer counted the American cruisers as destroyers, but the total number was correct. Another destroyer joined the fleet the next day.) On *Hiryu*'s bridge, Yamaguchi delivered final instructions to Lieutenants Joichi Tomonaga, Toshio Hashimoto, and Shigeru Mori, who were about to lead *Hiryu*'s second attack wave against the American fleet.

Joichi Tomonaga was one of three lieutenants to lead the second attack on Yorktown.

The first torpedoes hit the port side of the Yorktown *during the second attack by Japanese fighters.*

"Launch an attack upon other carriers than the one Kobayashi's group hit and set on fire," Yamaguchi said. "If no other carriers are found in the area, direct attack upon the same one." The admiral then shook hands with each pilot.

Lieutenant Commander Takashi Hashiguchi, *Hiryu*'s air officer, knew Tomonaga well and believed that Tomonaga blamed himself for the destruction the Americans had visited on *Kido Butai*. Tomonaga felt that because of his recommendation for a second strike on Midway, *Kido Butai*'s carriers had been caught defenseless while rearming the aircraft. Hashiguchi also knew that Tomonaga's airplane had been damaged during the Midway attack and still had a leak in its fuel tank. Apparently, Tomonaga was set on making a one-way mission against the Americans to atone for his guilt. Hashiguchi pitied Tomonaga's crew, who felt no such guilt but would go down with their pilot nonetheless.

"But at that time, the whole crew of *Hiryu*, including the fliers, had resolved to die for the Emperor and the motherland and so we didn't pay much attention to that," Hashiguchi confided. "Not only the fliers but the ship's crew actually did not concern themselves much with death, as we had determined to sink an enemy ship even if we had to ram into her."

Sixteen planes cleared *Hiryu*'s flight deck by 1245: five Kate torpedo bombers led by Tomonaga, five more under Hashimoto, and six Zeros commanded by Mori. *Yorktown*'s radar started tracking them from thirty-three miles out. Six Wildcats off *Yorktown*, already flying overhead cover, headed out to meet the approaching attack wave. Twelve more Wildcats climbed off *Yorktown*'s flight deck, half-refueled, to join the defense. By that time, *Yorktown* had been patched up, the wreckage had been cleared from the deck, and all four boilers were fired up and functioning. The rugged old carrier had some fighting left to do.

At 1432, Tomonaga radioed orders to his group: "Take positions in preparation for attack formation." Two minutes later, he commanded, "Entire force attack!" Tomonaga's Kates dove to the right, Hashimoto's to the left.

This time, five Japanese attackers slashed through American defenders and punishing antiaircraft fire to drop their torpedoes. *Yorktown* maneuvered out of the path of two torpedoes and a third torpedo missed, but two crashed home on the carrier's port side. Explosions rocked the fighting carrier, piercing fuel tanks, and flooding three fire rooms and the forward generator room, shutting down all electrical power. *Yorktown* stopped dead in the water again, then listed 17° to port. Within ten minutes, the list increased to 26°, with the luckless carrier's flight deck touching the water. It was time to get the crew to safety.

Yorktown Abandoned

At 1455, Captain Elliot Buckmaster said, "Pass the word along to abandon ship." Admiral Fletcher, watching from *Astoria*'s bridge, breathed a sigh of relief.

"I was biting my nails thinking that Captain Buckmaster made his decision to abandon ship too late," Fletcher said later. "Personally, I was . . . anxious at the time to get the boys off that ship. The saving of the lives of the officers and all of those fine young American boys was highly important to me."

As for the *Hiryu* strike force, half of it went into the water; five of ten Kates, three of six Zeros. Tomonaga's Kate took a hit just as he released his torpedo, and the airplane exploded into bits and pieces. Tomonaga would feel no more guilt.

A U.S. destroyer picks up Yorktown's *crew after the decision is made to abandon the heavily damaged ship.*

Task Force 16 Air Groups Attack *Hiryu*

Then the fickle face of battle smiled once more upon the Americans. Admiral Spruance had received a message from a *Yorktown* observation plane at 1445. Lieutenant Samuel Adams reported sighting *Hiryu*, 110 miles from *Yorktown* as of 1150, and steaming right at her.

At 1550, Spruance ordered all his remaining serviceable dive-bombers aloft right away. The group numbered twenty-four aircraft, a mix of planes from *Enterprise* and *Yorktown*. This time, Lieutenant W. Earl Gallaher took command, McClusky having been wounded in the arm during the earlier attack.

When his last Dauntless was in the air, Spruance sent a message to Fletcher: "TF 16 air groups are now striking the carrier which your search plane reported. . . . Have you any instructions for me?" Fletcher shot back an answer.

"None. Will conform to your movements."

Aboard *Hiryu*, by then about seventy-two miles away, Yamaguchi was preparing a third strike against the American carriers. He was in great spirits, mistakenly believing that his second attack wave had scored two hits on a second American carrier. The confusion arose when his pilots mistook the no longer burning *Yorktown* for a second carrier. At 1600, Yamaguchi reported to Nagumo: "Results obtained by second attack wave: Two certain torpedo hits on an *Enterprise* class carrier (not the same one as reported bombed)."

Forty-five minutes later, Gallaher's flight sighted *Hiryu* about thirty miles away. They could also see three columns of smoke rising from just over the horizon: three Japanese carriers dying a slow death. Once more, the American dive-bomber pilots arrived at just the right time, catching the fourth Japanese carrier in the process of rearming its remaining aircraft. While *Hiryu*'s tired pilots supped hurriedly on sweet rice balls, the Dauntlesses, loaded with 500- and 1,000-pound bombs, nosed over into their attack dives at 1700.

On *Hiryu*, a scout plane was just starting to take off, when, suddenly, a fearsome cry rang out: "Enemy dive-bombers overhead!"

Tomeo Kaku, *Hiryu*'s captain, ordered an immediate full right rudder and the carrier swerved sharply in an evasive starboard turn. The big vessel's swift maneuver threw off Gallaher's aim in the lead Dauntless, causing his bomb to drop harmlessly astern of *Hiryu*. Two more near misses followed. Then four 1,000-pound bombs struck in quick succession along the carrier's flight deck.

"Terrible sounds of explosions shook the vessel," recalled *Hiryu* command pilot Lieutenant Toshio Hashimoto, who had survived the second attack on *Yorktown*. And fleet photographer Teiichi Makishima remembered *Hiryu* burning from bow to stern but

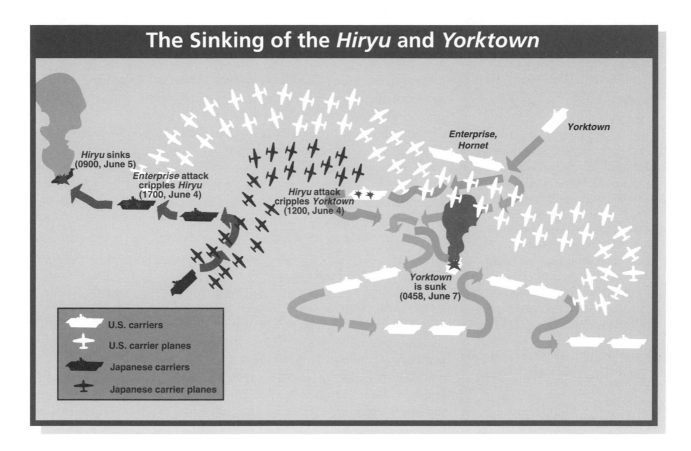

The Sinking of the *Hiryu* and *Yorktown*

Hiryu sinks
(0900, June 5)

Enterprise attack
cripples *Hiryu*
(1700, June 4)

Hiryu attack
cripples *Yorktown*
(1200, June 4)

Enterprise,
Hornet

Yorktown

Yorktown
is sunk
(0458, June 7)

U.S. carriers

U.S. carrier planes

Japanese carriers

Japanese carrier planes

"still running at high speed like a mad bull." As on the other three Japanese carriers, planes loaded with fuel and bombs caught fire and exploded, adding to the chaos and destruction. Now, all four of *Kido Butai's* carriers lay adrift in the water and burning.

The Dauntlesses of Gallaher's flight that still carried bombs then turned their attention to the battleship *Haruna*. But according to a Japanese report, they could manage only two "very near misses," one on either side of the ship. Defending Zeros scored two Dauntlesses during the attack.

Gallaher was just regrouping his flight to return to *Enterprise* when fifteen more Dauntlesses of Bombing and Scouting 8 off *Hornet* arrived on scene at 1712. The newcomers figured correctly that *Hiryu*, badly crippled and furiously ablaze, no longer represented a worthy target. They attacked the cruisers *Tone* and *Chikuma* instead but managed only two near misses, this time to port and starboard of *Tone*.

While *Hornet's* dive-bombers were still attacking *Tone*, at 1745, two groups of B-17s—one group from Midway,

The Japanese aircraft carrier Hiryu *is aflame after a successful bombing by the Americans.*

The *Bushido* Code

Throughout their history, the Japanese have endured local wars and lived in a warlike atmosphere. Members of the *daimyo* and *shogun* classes continually fought among themselves—feudal barons versus military governors—each supported by *samurai* (originally paid warriors; later, members of Japan's warrior class) and personal troops. The Japanese accordingly grew to admire the essential qualities of a good warrior and identified good citizenship as the embodiment of similar virtues. They gradually came to believe that those who did brave and noble acts in life would be rewarded with everlasting respect after death and an eternal resting place among their honored ancestors.

The *samurai* lived by a collection of principles that came to be known as the *Bushido* code, rules of conduct that governed their lives—and taught them how to die. Included in *Bushido* teachings were the disciplines of honor, courage, loyalty, enduring pain in silence, self-sacrifice, emperor worship, and disdain for death. *Bushido* principles crossed over lines of social class and became ingrained in Japanese culture.

This widespread adoption of martial ethics allowed ruling classes to rely on absolute obedience from much of the population. And total dedication to the *Bushido* code enabled many Japanese to meet death with courage and dignity.

the other from the Hawaiian island of Molokai—joined the attack. The heavy bombers enjoyed no more success in the late afternoon than they had in the early morning. When the Americans departed, a handful of *Hiryu*'s Zeros circled overhead, unable to land on the carrier's twisted deck. One by one, as their fuel ran out, they splashed into the sea.

Shortly after sunset, the eleven remaining dive-bombers of VMSB-241, led by Major Benjamin W. Norris, set out once more from Midway for another crack at the Japanese fleet. But heavy rain squalls arose to cancel any hope of finding the enemy. The American fliers were forced to cancel their search and return to Midway. Ten marines made it back. Major Norris did not.

The fighting of June 4 was over.

Down to the Sea

Soryu sank at 1915 with 718 men aboard. *Kaga* followed ten minutes later, carrying about 800 men to the bottom. *Akagi* burned through the night with 221 known dead aboard and was scuttled just before daybreak. *Hiryu* also burned through the night.

With the first rays of the rising sun breaking on the eastern horizon, Rear Admiral Tamon Yamaguchi assembled about eight hundred surviving crew members aboard *Hiryu* and announced:

> As commanding officer of this carrier division, I am fully and solely responsible for the loss of the *Hiryu* and *Soryu*. I shall remain on board to the end. I command all of you to leave the ship and continue your loyal service to His Majesty, the Emperor.

Dazed Japanese survivors from the aircraft carrier Hiryu *rest on the deck of the USS* Ballard. *The prisoners were found in a lifeboat after the Battle of Midway.*

Winged *Samurai*

The strict discipline and adherence to the Japanese warrior code implanted in these Japanese pilots made them tough opponents.

A tough new breed of *samurai* carried on Japan's warrior tradition during World War II. Saburo Sakai, the highest-scoring Japanese ace to survive that war, never forgot the harsh discipline of his early naval training:

> Whenever I committed a breach of discipline or an error in training, I was dragged physically from my cot by a petty officer.

> "Stand to the wall! Bend down, Recruit Sakai!" he would roar. "I am doing this to you, not because I hate you, but because I like you and want to make you a good seaman. *Bend down!*"

And with that he would swing a large stick of wood and with every ounce of strength he possessed would slam it against my upturned bottom. The pain was terrible, the force of the blows unremitting. There was no choice but to grit my teeth and struggle desperately not to cry out. At times I counted up to forty crashing impacts into my buttocks. Often I fainted from the pain. . . . The petty officer simply hurled a bucket of cold water over my prostrate form and bellowed for me to resume position, whereupon he continued his "discipline" until satisfied I would mend the error of my ways.

Such was the making of a *samurai*.

His staff asked to remain with him, but Yamaguchi ordered them off the ship also. Then *Hiryu*'s captain, Tomeo Kaku, tried to claim sole responsibility for going down with the ship. Kaku begged Yamaguchi to leave, but the admiral remained firm in his resolve, saying only, "The moon is so bright in the sky."

Kaku moved beside Yamaguchi and said, "We shall watch the moon together." And together they fulfilled the ancient Japanese warrior code of *Bushido*, which values honor above life.

The evacuation of all other officers and crew was completed at 0430 on June 5. The destroyer *Makigumo*, on Yamaguchi's orders, sent four torpedoes into the mortally wounded *Hiryu* at 0510. The last of *Kido Butai*'s carriers slipped beneath the waves at 0900.

Meanwhile, *Yorktown* clung to life, still listing 25° to port, but stable.

CHAPTER SIX

How It Ended

"The grim situation was painfully clear. Our air strength was wiped out. The enemy still had at least one carrier intact, we had failed to render the Midway airfields ineffective, and some of our ships were still in striking range of planes based there. With command of the air firmly in enemy hands, the outcome of the battle was a foregone conclusion."

—*Mitsuo Fuchida and Masatake Okumiya in* Midway

At 2130 on June 4, Vice Admiral Chuichi Nagumo, commander of *Kido Butai*, the First Carrier Striking Force, had sent a message to Admiral Isoroku Yamamoto, commander of the Combined Fleet: "Total enemy strength is five carriers, six heavy cruisers, and fifteen destroyers. They are steaming westward. We are retiring to the northwest escorting *Hiryu*. Speed, eighteen knots."

Several hundred miles to the northwest on the flagship *Yamato*, Chief of Staff of the Combined Fleet, Rear Admiral Matome Ugaki expressed contempt for Nagumo's message to Yamamoto: "The Nagumo force has no stomach for a night engagement. (Nagumo had in fact considered a night engagement but had thought better of it in the face of what he believed to be a superior enemy force.)

Yamamoto's stomach burned and churned with the acids born of high command, but he commenced preparations for a night battle at once. He had not given up hope of destroying the enemy fleet

Vice Admiral Nobutake Kondo replaced Nagumo as commander of Kido Butai.

and capturing Midway. Nagumo had already summoned help earlier that day from Rear Admiral Kakuji Kakuta's Second Carrier Striking Force (part of the Northern Force in the Aleutians). Kakuta replied that his carriers would join the Nagumo force off Midway on June 8. But Yamamoto felt that immediate action was needed. Yamamoto moved quickly to relieve Nagumo from command of *Kido Butai*, replacing him with Vice Admiral Nobutake Kondo, then commanding the Midway Invasion Force (Second Fleet). Kondo issued his first order to the "Night Action Force" at 2340 on June 4:

> (1) The Invasion Force Main Body [Kondo Force] will reach position 30° 28' N, 178° 35' W, 0300 June 5. Thereafter, searches will be made to the east in an effort to engage the enemy at night.

> (2) The First Carrier Striking Force [less *Hiryu*, *Akagi*, and their escorts] will reverse course immediately and participate in the night engagement. [Both Yamamoto and Kondo knew by this time that *Soryu* and *Kaga* had sunk, leaving only the badly damaged *Hiryu* and *Akagi* still afloat.]

Meanwhile, Admiral Raymond Spruance decided not to press his luck by pursuing the Japanese fleet. "I did not feel justified," he explained, "in risking a night encounter with possibly superior enemy forces, but on the other hand, I did not want to be too far away from Midway the next morning [June 5]. I wished to have a position from which either to follow up retreating enemy forces or to break up a landing attack on Midway." Spruance then reversed course in an evasive move to the east.

Operation Canceled

Because of Spruance's wise decision to move eastward, it soon became apparent to Yamamoto that it would be impossible to engage the enemy before dawn. Daybreak, of course, would find his ships once more at the mercy of American aircraft. Yamamoto and his staff considered various options.

The gunnery officer favored a night bombardment of Midway. Another staff officer insisted that the antiaircraft power of the Japanese battleships was sufficient to repel any attacks by American carrier planes. A face-saving plan for battleships, including *Yamato* to bombard Midway in broad daylight on June 5 was then submitted to Chief of Staff Ugaki. Perhaps recalling that naval history teaches never to fight against land forces with naval vessels, Ugaki curtly dismissed the plan in these terms:

> The stupidity of engaging such shore installations with a surface force ought to be clear to you. The airfield on Midway is still usable, a large number of planes is based there, and some

Nagumo's Mistakes

Battles are often won simply on the basis of which side makes fewer mistakes. In their analysis of the Japanese defeat at Midway, Mitsuo Fuchida and Masatake Okumiya wrote: "Indeed, from a study of the operations of the American as well as the Japanese forces, it is hard not to acknowledge that *all* the errors in this action were committed on our side.

"That Admiral Nagumo was guilty of most of these does not warrant the conclusion that he was less competent than the other force commanders. It was his misfortune, because the Nagumo Force was the only Japanese force actually to come to grips with the enemy. . . . It now appears, with the benefit of hindsight, that Admiral Nagumo committed three serious blunders.

"The first of these was his failure to enforce adequate search dispositions on the morning of the Midway strike. Had he employed an earlier, two-phase search, the unsuspected enemy task force would probably have been discovered soon enough to permit Nagumo to strike the first blow instead of taking it.

"Nagumo's second mistake had to do with the method he employed in dividing up his carrier planes between the first and second attack waves. . . . Had Nagumo launched his Midway strike from just two carriers and held the other two in reserve, ready for any eventuality, he would not have found his hands tied at the critical moment of the battle.

"The third and perhaps gravest error committed by Nagumo was his failure, as soon as it was discovered that the enemy task force included a carrier, to launch immediately all available planes for an attack, whether properly armed or not and even if fighter protection could not be provided. . . . Yamaguchi's judgment [to launch an immediate air strike] in this crucial situation was the only correct one. Nagumo chose what seemed to him the orthodox and safer course, and from that moment his carriers were doomed."

of the enemy carriers are still intact. Our battleships, for all their fire power, would be destroyed by enemy air and submarine attacks before we could even get close enough to use our big guns.

If circumstances permit, we will be able to launch another offensive after the Second Carrier Striking Force [Kakuta] has joined. But even if that proves impossible and we must accept defeat in this operation, we will not have lost the war.

Until then, no one had even considered—let alone voiced— the idea that the previously unbeatable navy of Japan might suffer a defeat. After a short silence, one of the officers asked, "But how can we apologize to His Majesty for this defeat?"

Admiral Yamamoto, who had kept quiet during the discussions, then cut in sharply and said, "Leave that to me. I am the only one who must apologize to His Majesty." At 0255, June 5,

Admiral Isoroku Yamamoto began life as an orphan, only to become the central figure in the Japanese navy. Yamamoto was killed in action when his plane was shot down by American fighters in 1943.

Yamamoto issued the order that sealed Japan's defeat at Midway; the first sentence stated: *The Midway Operation is canceled.*

Just *declaring* an end to the action did not end it, however, as the Americans were now pressing the attack. The fighting would continue for two more days.

In Pursuit of the Enemy

Only an hour after Yamamoto canceled the Midway Operation, Lieutenant Commander John W. Murphy Jr., skipper of the American submarine *Tambor,* reported sighting "many unidentified ships" about eighty-nine miles west of Midway and heading away from the base. Murphy had discovered a Japanese force of four cruisers and two destroyers that Admiral Kondo had sent to bombard Midway at night. When Yamamoto's cancellation order came through, the six warships, under the command of Rear Admiral Takeo Kurita, turned away from Midway and steamed northwest. Running on the surface in the dark, *Tambor* started tracking them.

The Japanese spotted the American submarine at daybreak and took immediate evasive and offensive actions. *Tambor* crash-dived. In the flurry of emergency maneuvers, the cruiser *Mogami* rammed the cruiser *Mikuma*. Both cruisers sustained damages—*Mogami*, which lost part of her bow, most severely—forcing both cruisers to reduce speed to twelve knots. At 0630, a patrolling PBY from Midway mistakenly reported "two battleships streaming oil." A half-hour later, the marines of VMSB-241 managed to put twelve dive-bombers in the air. Six Dauntlesses led by Captain Marshall A. Tyler and six Vindicators under Captain Richard E. Fleming roared aloft from Midway to hunt down the enemy "battleships."

Tyler's group located the sister ships *Mikuma* and *Mogami* forty-five minutes into their search. Tyler led his pilots down in a plunging attack on *Mogami*, but they could do no better than a few near misses. A few minutes behind Tyler's Dauntlesses, Fleming's Vindicators arrived on scene, as did a flight of B-17s from Midway commanded by Lieutenant Colonel Brooke Allen.

Fleming took his Vindicators down in a glide-bombing attack on *Mikuma*. Fleming managed to release his bomb, but his machine burst into flames. Flying full out, Fleming crashed into a gun turret just aft of *Mikuma*'s bridge. It is not known whether his last act was intentional. Captain Akira Soji of *Mogami* looked on.

"Very brave," Soji said to himself, convinced that he had just witnessed an American suicide attack. Fleming's crash did more damage than any of the near misses. Kurita's cruiser force then continued their limping withdrawal to the northwest.

Mortal Wounds

Meanwhile, Fletcher still held out hope that *Yorktown* might be rescued from a watery grave. With the esteemed old carrier still standing steady at a 25° list, Fletcher directed Lieutenant Commander Donald J. Ramsey, skipper of the destroyer *Hughes*, to "stand by *Yorktown*. Do not permit anyone to board her. Sink her if necessary to prevent capture or if serious fire develops."

At noon on June 5, the minesweeper *Vireo* arrived and took *Yorktown* in tow. A volunteer salvage crew boarded *Yorktown* and started work and soon began to correct her list. While work continued, *Vireo* towed the stricken carrier slowly toward Pearl Harbor, escorted by the destroyers *Hammann*, *Benham*, and *Balch*. By 1330 the next day, it started to look as though *Yorktown* would once again be returned from a near-death experience.

Then suddenly a lookout cried, "Torpedoes!"

Four white streaks shot through the water, heading straight at *Hammann* and *Yorktown*. The first missed its mark. But the second exploded against *Hammann*'s side, breaking the destroyer's spine. *Hammann* sank almost immediately, exploding when she hit bottom and killing two swimmers. The third and fourth torpedoes struck the unfortunate *Yorktown* on her starboard side,

The Japanese heavy cruiser Mikuma *under attack by American dive-bombers.*

opening up huge holes in her steel plates. Nothing could save her this time.

Earlier, the Japanese submarine I-168, commanded by Lieutenant Yahashi Tanabe, had been sent by Yamamoto to "shell and destroy enemy air base on Eastern Island." When *Yorktown* was seen later by a Japanese search plane, Yamamoto redirected Tanabe to attack the carrier. The I-168 had proceeded then to execute the only decisive Japanese naval action during the Battle of Midway.

Last Strikes

On June 6, Admiral Spruance launched the final air strikes of the Battle of Midway. Task Force 16 had pursued the retreating Japanese fleet to a position about 340 miles northwest of Midway. At 0510, *Enterprise* dispatched eighteen scout aircraft to search a 200-mile-wide span of ocean to the west. They contacted Kurita's retreating cruiser force (one carrier, two heavy cruisers, and eight destroyers) at about 0645 in two separate sightings. The day's first strike lifted off *Hornet* at 0757, followed by a second from *Enterprise* at 1045, and a final strike from *Hornet* at 1330.

Even though the Japanese had called off the Midway attack, fierce fighting continued for two more days. At top, troops watch as the USS Hammann *sinks before their eyes. (Right) Planes from the* Hornet *bomb and strafe a Japanese cruiser.*

Death of a Near-God

On April 14, 1943, at 0802, Captain Edwin T. Layton, the Pacific Fleet intelligence officer at Pearl Harbor, reported the latest intelligence message to Admiral Chester W. Nimitz. "Our old friend, Yamamoto," Layton said, handing the message to his superior. "Do we try to get him?"

The message reported that Admiral Isoroku Yamamoto was scheduled to fly from Rabaul at 0600, April 18, on an inspection tour of Ballalae Island in the Solomons. Yamamoto's flight would comprise a medium bomber (later two bombers) escorted by six Zero fighters. Nimitz read the message and smiled at Layton. "Do we try to get him?"

Admiral Nimitz thought it over and said, "All right, we'll try it." He then notified Admiral William F. Halsey, who was in the Solomons, to "initiate preliminary planning."

Nimitz next asked for and received approval of the mission from Secretary of the Navy Frank Knox and President Franklin D. Roosevelt. Yamamoto's flight arrived over Kahili airfield on Ballalae at 0934 on April 18. It was met by sixteen U.S. Air Force P-38 Lightning fighters from Henderson Field on Guadalcanal.

The first P-38s to return to Guadalcanal performed barrel rolls over Henderson Field. Shortly thereafter, Admiral Halsey received the following message:

POP GOES THE WEASEL. P-38'S LED BY MAJOR JOHN W. MITCHELL USA VISITED KAHILI AREA ABOUT 0930. SHOT DOWN TWO BOMBERS ESCORTED BY ZEROS FLYING CLOSE FORMATION. ONE SHOT BELIEVED TO BE TEST FLIGHT. THREE ZEROS ADDED TO SCORE SUM TOTAL SIX. ONE P-38 FAILED TO RETURN. APRIL 18 SEEMS TO BE OUR DAY.

The great Yamamoto—architect of both the Pearl Harbor attack and the Battle of Midway—was dead.

At 0930, twenty-six Dauntlesses and eight Wildcats from *Hornet* sighted the crippled cruisers *Mikuma* and *Mogami*, escorted by the destroyers *Arashio* and *Asashio*. Over target, Commander Stanhope Ring ordered his pilots to "Attack when ready."

Lieutenant William J. "Gus" Widhelm replied, "Widhelm is ready. Prepare the Japs."

The attack commenced at 0950. Ring's *Hornet* group scored two hits on *Mogami*, two or three on *Mikuma,* and one on *Asashio*. One Dauntless went down from antiaircraft fire. The remaining aircraft returned to the carrier to rearm.

Lieutenant Walter C. Short led the *Enterprise* attack group, consisting of thirty-one dive-bombers, twelve fighters, and three torpedo bombers. They struck the same cruiser group at about 1230. A transcript of the colorful pilot exchanges over the radio sums up the action that followed:

"Your bomb really hit on the fantail. Boy, that's swell!"

"Look at that [bleep-bleep] burn!"

"Hit the [bleep-bleep] again!"

"Let's hit them all."

"Put all of them smack on the bottom."

"Let's get a couple of those destroyers."

"These Japs are easy as shooting ducks in a rain barrel."

"Tojo, you [bleep-bleep], send out the rest and we'll get those too!" And so on.

Wally Short's pilots delivered two more hits on *Mogami* and really unloaded on *Mikuma*, scoring at least five direct hits. A few Dauntlesses absorbed some minor damage from antiaircraft fire, but all returned safely to *Enterprise*.

Ring's *Hornet* group returned with a second load at 1445. By then, of course, both cruisers were badly battered. The *Hornet* group ripped into them one last time, scoring another hit apiece on *Mikuma* and *Arashio* before turning for home. *Mogami* avoided any further hits. All American aircraft again made it home safely.

On his return, Ring reported: "Very heavy explosions were seen in the CA [heavy cruiser], and it was left completely gutted by fire, personnel abandoning ship."

Endings

As the sun dipped below the western horizon on June 6, *Mikuma* rolled over on her port side and slipped beneath the waves. Her three battered companions managed to limp off to safety, but *Mogami* would not see action again for another year.

The Japanese cruiser Mikuma *sinks on the afternoon of June 6, 1942, after successful attacks by fighters from the USS* Enterprise.

Another *Yorktown*

After *Yorktown* slipped beneath the waves at 0458 on June 7, 1942, Captain Elliot Buckmaster, her skipper, returned to Pearl Harbor and sadly submitted this report to Admiral Nimitz:

> During all these actions and the many weeks at sea in preparation for them the fighting spirit of YORKTOWN was peerless; that fighting spirit remains alive even though the ship herself has perished gloriously in battle. The wish closest to the hearts of all of us who were privileged to serve in that gallant ship is that she be preserved not only in memory but by the crew's being kept together to man, commission, and return against the enemy a new aircraft carrier, preferably another YORKTOWN.

Listing heavily to port and with her guns still pointing defiantly upward, the Yorktown *slowly sinks into the sea.*

At daybreak on June 7, officers and men lined the decks aboard *Yorktown*'s escort vessels and looked on sadly as she began to list more sharply. Flags rode at half-mast. The inevitable was about to happen. At 0458, in the words of *Yorktown*'s skipper Captain Elliot Buckmaster, "she turned over on her port side and sank in two thousand fathoms of water, with all her battle flags flying." As her bow disappeared into the sea, all hands stood at attention and saluted. And grown men cried without shame.

The Battle of Midway was over.

AFTERWORD

Rising Sun Setting

Rear Admiral Raymond A. Spruance halted his westward pursuit of the enemy on June 7, 1942. With his ships running low on fuel and reaching a point of overextension, he ordered their return to Pearl Harbor. He could ask no more of them.

The Japanese Combined Fleet under Admiral Isoroku Yamamoto stood defeated in the Pacific for the first time during World War II. Yamamoto's fleet lost 4 aircraft carriers, 1 heavy

A heavily damaged Japanese cruiser lists before plunging into a watery grave.

"Midway to Our Objective"

The June 6, 1942, evening edition of the Honolulu *Star-Bulletin* proudly hailed the American victory at Midway. "They Wanted To Know, 'Where's The U.S. Pacific Fleet?' Did They?" it asked; then followed with: "Admiral Nimitz Had the Answer and It Has Been Delivered at Midway."

Bold black headlines declared: MIDWAY BATTLE TOLL: JAPANESE SHIPS SUNK! Beneath the headlines, the paper printed Nimitz's first battle report at 1245:

> Through the skill and devotion to duty of our armed forces of all branches in the Midway area, our citizens can now rejoice that a momentous victory is in the making.

It was on Sunday just six months ago that the Japanese made their peacetime attack on our fleet and army activities on Oahu. . . .

Pearl Harbor has now been partially avenged. Vengeance will not be complete until Japanese sea power has been reduced to impotence.

We have made substantial progress in that direction.

The admiral could not resist adding, "Perhaps we will be forgiven if we claim we are about midway to our objective."

---

cruiser, and 275 planes; 3,500 men were killed. The loss of the carriers had the effect of removing Japan's offensive initiative, forcing the country to fight a defensive war from that point on.

The most decisive naval victory in American history came at the cost of 1 aircraft carrier, 1 destroyer, 132 land- and carrier-based planes, and 307 American lives.

Of the stunning American victory at Midway, Captain Edwin T. Layton, the Pacific Fleet intelligence officer, later wrote:

> At Midway the Japanese lost or left behind a naval air force that had been the terror of the Pacific—an élite force, an overwhelming force that would never again come back and spread destruction and fear as it had over the first six months of the war. This was the meaning of Midway.

A later, in-depth study at the U.S. Naval War College enlarged on the significance of the Midway victory and its effect on the course of the Pacific war:

> [I]t had a stimulating effect on the morale of the American fighting forces; . . . it stopped the Japanese expansion to the east; it put an end to Japanese offensive action which had been all conquering for the first six months of the war; it restored the balance of naval power in the Pacific which thereafter steadily

The Importance of the Aircraft Carrier

Although Great Britain introduced the aircraft carrier to naval action during World War I, it was not until a generation later that the carrier displaced the battleship as the capital ship of the fleet. But carrier-based torpedo bombers and dive-bombers demonstrated their effectiveness against surface ships immediately at the onset of the Second World War. And it soon became clear to naval strategists that control of the air translated into control of the seas, regardless of the relative size of opposing fleets.

The magnificent American victory in the Battle of Midway removed all doubt about the aircraft carrier's mastery in sea engagements. Rather than mere supporters of naval ships of the line, carrier-based planes demonstrated that they were in fact the primary naval striking force. The airplane now extended naval firepower for hundreds of miles beyond the range of naval gunfire. No longer would the vaunted battlewagon reign supreme in contested waters of the world. At Midway, the battleship surrendered its crown as "queen of battle" without a struggle to the aircraft carrier.

Aircraft carriers revolutionized battle strategy.

shifted to favor the American side; and it removed the threat to Hawaii and to the west coast of the United States. . . .

CinC Combined Fleet [Admiral Yamamoto] desired to fight a decisive naval action with the American fleet at the earliest possible moment and before American construction could overwhelm the Japanese fleet by sheer force of numbers. He was now forced to give up the idea of holding such a fleet engagement at an early date and in remote waters. He was instead forced to wait until the Americans took the offensive, and owing to the loss of his carriers he was restricted to waters much nearer the [Japanese] Empire. Thus it was that the Japanese were forced to a defensive role.

Without regard to right of cause, purity of purpose, or end result, may it long be remembered that men on both sides fought with great dedication and died with extraordinary courage. Honor to them all.

Two months to the day after the Battle of Midway ended, the United States launched its first offensive operation of the war. The marines landed at Guadalcanal in the Solomons on August 7, 1942. Their amphibious assault against the Japanese island stronghold marked the beginning of the setting of the Rising Sun.

Glossary

aft: Rear.

Allies: Allied nations aligned against the Axis powers during World War II, including the United States, Great Britain, France, the USSR, and others.

annihilate: Completely destroy; wipe out.

armada: Fleet of warships.

assassination: Murder, especially of a politically important person, either for monetary or fanatical motives.

astern: At or toward the rear of a ship; behind a ship.

Axis: Military alliance formed by Germany, Italy, and Japan during World War II.

Banzai!:   Japanese battle cry; original meaning "May you live forever!"

battlewagon: Battleship.

bearing: Compass direction.

bow: The extreme forward part of a ship.

Bushido: The code of conduct of the _samurai_ of Japan, embracing the virtues of courage, self-discipline, courtesy, gentleness, and keeping one's word.

calculated risk: Military principle of avoiding exposure of a friendly force to a superior enemy force unless there is reasonable assurance that such exposure will result in inflicting greater harm on the enemy force.

China Clipper: American flying boat that established first scheduled airline flights across the Pacific in the 1930s.

China Incident: Japanese invasion of China in 1937.

CinCPAC: Commander in chief of the U.S. Pacific Fleet.

daimyo: A Japanese feudal baron.

ditching: Forced landing at sea.

dive-bombing: A steep-dive (hell-diving) bombing approach.

Eastern Island: The smaller of the two main islands of Midway Atoll (_see also_ Sand Island).

emperor: Ruler of an empire, as Emperor Hirohito of Japan (1926–89).

fantail: Aft end of a ship.

fathom: Unit of measure equal to six feet.

feint: Mock attack made in one place to distract attention from the main attack coming elsewhere; a diversion.

feudal: Of, relating to, or suggestive of feudalism.

feudalism: A political or social system based on the holding of land by giving fees and services to the landowner.

flagship: Ship that carries an admiral and flies his flag.

flattop: Aircraft carrier.

flying boat: A seaplane with a hull designed for floating.

forward: At or toward the front of a ship.

glide-bombing: Dive-bombing by a shallow approach.

Greater East Asia Co-Prosperity Sphere: Japanese policy that called for the recognition of economic and political ties between Japan and the "Southern Regions."

grid location: Geographical location defined by an intersection of latitude and longitude lines on a map.

havoc: Widespread destruction; great disorder.

intercept: Head off.

kamikaze: Literally, divine wind; member of a Japanese air attack corps during World War II assigned to make a suicidal crash on a target (as a ship).

Kido Butai: Carrier Striking Force.

"Kimigayo":   The Japanese national anthem.

Kodo-Ha: The Way of the Emperor; a Japanese political movement that supported a totalitarian state controlled by the army.

monsoon: Periodic wind, especially in the Indian Ocean and southern Asia; a season associated with the wind, usually marked by heavy rains.

New Order in Europe: National Socialism (Nazism); the system of economic, social, and political control that prevailed in Germany and its subject nations during the Second World War.

New Order in Greater East Asia: Japanese version of Germany's New Order that proposed a policy of "Asia for Asians."

Operation MI: Japanese plan to occupy Midway Atoll and defeat the U.S. Pacific Fleet.

Pearl Harbor: U.S. naval installation at Oahu, Hawaii; headquarters of the U.S. Pacific Fleet.

perimeter: Line or strip bounding or protecting an area; outer limits.

pickle: Torpedo.

Point Luck: Grid location about 325 miles northeast of Midway; designated by Admiral Nimitz as the rendezvous point for U.S. Naval Task Forces 16 and 17 prior to the Battle of Midway.

port: Left-hand side.

reconnaissance: Preliminary search to gain information, especially for military purposes.

samurai: Military retainer of a Japanese *daimyo* practicing the warrior code of *Bushido*; the warrior upper class of Japan.

Sand Island: The larger of the two main islands at Midway Atoll (*see also* Eastern Island).

scuttle: To let water into a ship in order to sink it.

shogun: One of a line of military governors who ruled Japan until the revolution of 1867–68.

simultaneous: Existing or happening at the same time.

Sino-: Chinese.

Southern Regions: Southeast Asian nations rich in raw materials, including the East Indies, Malaya, the Philippines, Java, Sumatra, Burma (now Myanmar), and Thailand.

staff: Body of officers assisting a commanding officer and concerned with the operation of a military unit as a whole; a member of such a body is called a staff officer.

starboard: Right-hand side.

strategy: The planning and directing of the entire operation of a war or campaign (*see also* tactics).

tactics: The art of placing or maneuvering forces skillfully in a battle (*see also* strategy).

totalitarian: Of or relating to a state-controlled government.

Tripartite Pact: Formal agreement that formed a military alliance between Germany, Italy, and Japan during World War II; the three nations became known as the Axis powers, or simply the Axis.

Two Hares: Conflicting goals, as a hunter trying to chase two hares at the same time.

V: Heavier than air.

VB: Bombing Squadron.

VF: Fighting Squadron.

victory fever: Exaggerated sense of well-being and overconfidence experienced by the Japanese following a series of easy early victories at the start of World War II.

VMF: Marine Fighting Squadron.

VMSB: Marine Scout-Bombing Squadron.

VT: Torpedo Squadron.

VS: Scouting Squadron.

For Further Reading

A. Barker, *Midway: The Turning Point*. New York: Ballantine Books, 1971. A fast-paced retelling of the battle that turned back the Japanese at Midway.

Thomas B. Buell, *The Quiet Warrior: A Biography of Admiral Raymond A. Spruance*. Boston: Little, Brown, 1974. An in-depth portrait of the U.S. naval commander most responsible for America's miraculous victory at Midway.

Robert J. Casey, *Torpedo Junction: With the Pacific Fleet from Pearl Harbor to Midway*. New York: Bobbs-Merrill, 1942. A personal reminiscence of the first six months of the naval war in the Pacific by a noted war correspondent and author.

Winston S. Churchill, *The Hinge of Fate*. Boston: Houghton Mifflin, 1950. The former British prime minister's marvelous recounting of the Second World War from January 1942 through May 1943, emphasizing the Pacific war during its most crucial period.

George H. Gay, *Sole Survivor*. Naples, FL: Naples Ad/Graphics Services, 1976. The only survivor of Torpedo Squadron 8 tells his story.

Edwin P. Hoyt, *The Glory of the Solomons*. New York: Stein and Day, 1983. An interesting overview of the United States on the offensive in the South Pacific, shortly after the decisive battle at Midway. A section devoted to Admiral Yamamoto's continuing strategies and death soon after this major Japanese defeat is of particular interest.

Samuel Eliot Morison, *History of United States Naval Operations in World War II,* Vol. IV, *Coral Sea, Midway, and Submarine Actions*. Boston: Little, Brown, 1950. The definitive work on the Coral Sea and Midway engagements by an esteemed historian.

Zenji Orita with Joseph D. Harrington, *I-Boat Captain*. Canoga Park, CA: Major Books, 1978. A Japanese submarine captain writes about the undersea war in the Pacific, including a periscoped view of the Midway battle and the sinking of *Yorktown*.

E.B. Potter, *Nimitz*. Annapolis, MD: Naval Institute Press, 1976. The story of Admiral Chester W. Nimitz, who commanded all U.S. naval services, sea and air, in the Pacific theater during World War II.

Gordon W. Prange, with Donald L. Goldstein and Katherine V. Dillon, *At Dawn We Slept: The Untold Story of Pearl Harbor*. New York: McGraw-Hill, 1981. The classic account of the Japanese attack on Pearl Harbor that forced America's entry into World War II and led to the Battle of Midway six months later.

Works Consulted

J. Bryan III, "Midway: Turning Point in the Pacific," in R*eader's Digest Illustrated Story of World War II*. Pleasantville, NY: The Reader's Digest Association, 1969. A concise yet comprehensive account of the carrier battle at Midway that changed the course of the Pacific war.

Harold L. Buell, *Dauntless Helldivers: A Dive-Bomber Pilot's Epic Story of the Carrier Battles*. New York: Bantam Doubleday Dell Publishing Group, 1991. A decorated navy pilot and noted historian relates a personal account of dive-bomber action during World War II, including the Coral Sea and Midway engagements.

Robert J. Cressman et al., *A Glorious Page in Our History: The Battle of Midway 4–6 June 1942.* Missoula, MT: Pictorial Histories Publishing Company, 1990. A thoroughly documented, profusely illustrated account of the Midway encounter.

R. Ernest Dupuy and Trevor N. Dupuy, *The Encyclopedia of Military History.* New York: Harper & Row, 1977. A monumental work on warfare by two noted historians; includes a keen analysis of the Battle of Midway and its effect on the Pacific war.

Mitsuo Fuchida and Masatake Okumiya, *Midway: The Battle That Doomed Japan, the Japanese Navy's Story.* Annapolis, MD: Naval Institute Press, 1955. A valuable account of the battle as seen through the eyes of two Japanese naval officers who took part in the engagement.

William Green, *Famous Fighters of the Second World War*, rev. ed. New York: Doubleday and Company, 1976. A well-researched volume depicting some of the great fighters of World War II.

Jiro Horikoshi, *Eagles of Mitsubishi: The Story of the Zero Fighter.* Translated by Shojiro Shindo and Harold N. Wantiez. Seattle: University of Washington Press, 1981. The design, development, and service of the Zero fighter as told by the aircraft's designer.

Rikihei Inoguchi and Tadashi Nakajima, with Roger Pineau, *The Divine Wind: Japan's Kamikaze Force in World War II.* New York: Ballantine Books, 1958. Two former members of Japan's suicide squadrons and an esteemed American naval historian relive the tragic ten-month history of the *kamikaze* attack force.

Edward Jablonski, *Airwar.* Vol. I. Garden City, NY: Doubleday, 1971. A history of aerial warfare during World War II; contains an excellent chapter on the Midway battle, including some great photographs of the action.

Walter Lord, *Incredible Victory.* New York: HarperCollins, 1993. A fascinating account of the American victory at Midway, told in alternating chapters of the advance of the Japanese fleet and of the desperate defense of the Americans.

Bernard Millot, *Divine Thunder: The Life and Death of the Kamikazes.* New York: Pinnacle Books, 1970. A fascinating account of Japan's suicide pilots and their devastating assaults against Allied forces in World War II. The author is a French aviation journalist and historian.

Masatake Okumiya and Jiro Horikoshi, with Martin Caidin, *Zero!* New York: Ballantine Books, 1956. The story of Japan's air war in the Pacific by the Japanese commander of many of its sea-air battles and the designer of the famous fighter; includes insightful text on the Japanese view of the Midway battle.

Gordon W. Prange, with Donald M. Goldstein and Katherine V. Dillon, *Miracle at Midway*. New York: Penguin Books, 1983. A sweeping narrative that shows how American strategies and decisions led to a stunning American victory and a crushing Japanese defeat at Midway.

Clark G. Reynolds and the Editors of Time-Life Books, *The Carrier War*. Alexandria, VA: Time-Life Books, 1982. A well-written and beautifully illustrated history of carrier warfare in the Second World War, including an excellent chapter on the Battle of Midway.

William L. Shirer, *The Rise and Fall of the Third Reich: A History of Nazi Germany*. New York: Simon & Schuster, 1959. This classic, by a highly regarded foreign correspondent and historian, contains valuable insight into the German-Italian-Japanese Axis during World War II.

John Toland, *But Not in Shame*. New York: New American Library of World Literature, 1961. A remarkable history of the crucial first six months of the Pacific war, including vivid accounts of the carrier battles in the Coral Sea and at Midway.

———, *The Rising Sun*. New York: Random House, 1970. A narrative history of modern Japan from the invasion of Manchuria and China to the atom bomb; includes a fine account of the Japanese navy's showdown battle with the American fleet at Midway.

Appendix 1: Brief Biographies

Admiral Isoroku Yamamoto (born Takano) rose from modest beginnings as an orphan to become the central figure in the Japanese navy at the start of the Pacific war. As commander in chief of the Combined Fleet, he was looked to for naval leadership above all others as Japan moved toward war with the United States.

A graduate of the Imperial Naval Academy, he was further educated in the United States, majoring in the study of oil at Harvard. As a promising young naval officer, he served as a naval attaché in Washington during 1925–27. He grew to like Americans, baseball, bridge, and poker. More important, he developed a keen sense of America's huge industrial potential.

Yamamoto served as navy minister during 1936–39. He was made chief of Naval Aviation Headquarters in 1938 and held both positions until promoted to commander of the First Fleet in 1940. Known as "the father of Japanese aviation," Yamamoto was said to possess the sharpest mind in the Japanese navy.

Fully aware of America's industrial power, Yamamoto opposed a war with the United States. In light of existing U.S. naval strength and a shortage of raw materials (mainly oil) on the part of his own nation, he warned that the Japanese fleet could not fight successfully for more than a year.

Nevertheless, Yamamoto, always a gambler, originated the bold concept of attacking Pearl Harbor in early 1941 and oversaw the planning and execution of the operation. He then, at age fifty-six, conceived the plan for the assault on Midway, Operation MI. Yamamoto's failure to concentrate the full power of his Combined Fleet at Midway contributed more than any other single factor to Japan's ringing defeat.

Isoroku Yamamoto was killed when his plane was shot down by American fighters near Bougainville on April 18, 1943, while he was traveling to visit Japanese forces on Short-land Island.

Vice Admiral Chuichi Nagumo, commander of the First Carrier Striking Force (*Kido Butai*), ranked right next to Yamamoto as a central figure in the Japanese navy as it prepared for the Pacific war. Also an Imperial Naval Academy graduate, Nagumo held several cruiser commands and led a destroyer squadron before serving as captain of the battleship *Yamashiro* in 1934.

Nagumo achieved the rank of rear admiral in 1935 and was promoted to vice admiral in 1939. Appointed commander of the First Air Fleet in April 1941, he assumed operational control of six carriers and directed the Japanese attack on Pearl Harbor. In March 1942 he led a sweep of the Indian Ocean that temporarily drove the British navy from the sea with only light Japanese losses.

Despite his successes, Nagumo never felt comfortable as an aviation commander and relied heavily on the advice of his chief air planner, Commander Minoru Genda. As leader of *Kido Butai*, Nagumo faltered at a critical point during the Battle of Midway and suffered the loss of all four of his carriers. Although he deserves some criticism for Japan's defeat at Midway, it must be acknowledged that he was saddled with a clumsy plan and encountered American opposition of unexpected strength.

Chuichi Nagumo commanded a six-thousand-man, land-based naval force during the American invasion of Saipan, but committed suicide in the final stages of the battle (July 8–13, 1944).

Commander Minoru Genda, operations officer, First Carrier Division, graduated from the Imperial Naval Academy in 1924. He went on to train in carrier aviation and became a pilot aboard *Akagi* in 1931. After graduating from Naval Staff College, where he was known as "Madman Genda" because of his belief in the primary role of naval air power, he became a flight instructor at the naval training center in Yokosuka. Genda next served as assistant naval attaché in London during 1938–40, after which he was promoted to commander in 1940 and made operation officer, First Carrier Division, under Admiral Nagumo.

While serving under Nagumo, Genda drafted the first detailed plans for the attack on Pearl Harbor. He played a key role in developing the shallow-running torpedo attacks used at Pearl Harbor. In addition to taking part in the Pearl Harbor attack, Genda served Nagumo in the Indian Ocean and at Midway.

After Midway, Genda saw further action in the Solomons and the Santa Cruz Islands in the South Pacific. He was promoted to captain and assigned to the naval air defenses of Japan's home islands in 1945. Genda retired as chief of staff, Air Self-Defense Force, in 1962. Although he often stepped to a different drumbeat, few officers could equal his achievements as an air commander and as a tactical planner.

Minoru Genda died in Tokyo on August 15, 1989.

Admiral Chester William Nimitz, commander in chief, U.S. Pacific Fleet (CinCPAC), and commander of all naval forces in the sea and in the air in the Pacific theater, provided the strategic direction and driving force behind America's victory at Midway. He went on to play a principal leadership role during the victorious American advance across the central Pacific, successfully maintaining his command until the end of the war.

Nimitz attended the U.S. Naval Academy during 1901–05 and received his ensign's commission on China station in 1907. He served as chief of staff to the commander of the Atlantic Fleet's submarine division during World War I. He later held several key staff positions in the Atlantic Fleet, served as commander of a submarine division (1929–31), and captained the cruiser *Augusta* (1931–33).

Promoted to rear admiral in 1938, Nimitz commanded a cruiser division and a battleship division before being appointed chief of staff of the Bureau of Navigation in June 1939. After Admiral Husband E. Kimmel resigned in December 1941, Nimitz assumed command of the Pacific Fleet in Pearl Harbor and was promoted to admiral shortly thereafter.

An officer of vast experience, Nimitz kept an open mind at all times and excelled at accomplishing his goals without angering or upsetting his fellow officers. But he wanted the right person in the right job and would not hesitate to replace anyone who was not up to his expectations. He made sound decisions and carried them out swiftly. His performance in a most difficult job at a most difficult time in America's history remains a model for all those who follow. Americans shall long stand in his debt.

Chester W. Nimitz died near San Francisco on February 20, 1966.

Rear Admiral Frank Jack Fletcher, commander of Task Force 17, and overall commander of Task Forces 16 and 17 at sea during the Battle of Midway, graduated from the U.S. Naval Academy in 1906 and was commissioned an ensign in 1908.

Fletcher received the Medal of Honor for his rescue of refugees aboard the S.S. *Esperanza* during the Veracruz (Mexico) landing in 1914. He commanded the destroyer *Benham* on submarine patrol in the Atlantic Fleet during World War I, then saw action in the brief Philippine uprising in 1924.

After attending both the Naval and Army War Colleges, he served as aide to the secretary of the navy (1933–36), commanded the battleship *New Mexico* (1936–38), and served in the Bureau of Personnel (1938–39), where he was promoted to rear admiral and given command of a cruiser division in the Atlantic Fleet.

In December 1941 he commanded the Wake Island relief force aboard the carrier *Saratoga* (arriving too late). He next directed Task Force 17 aboard *Yorktown* during the Battle of the Coral Sea in early May 1942, before assuming sea command of Task Forces 16 and 17 at Midway in late May. He moved on to command the carrier force at the invasion of Guadalcanal and Tulagi (August 7, 1942) and later fought Yamamoto's fleet to a draw in the Eastern Solomons (August 23–25). Appointed to command of the naval forces in the North Pacific in 1943, he served there until the war ended.

A large, likable man, Fletcher was a widely experienced officer, often thought of as a "sailor's sailor." In that he felt unfamiliar with aircraft carriers, he tended to exercise caution. History has judged his performance at Midway as adequate but not brilliant. But he always did his duty as he saw it and to the best of his ability. He well deserves his country's praise.

Frank Jack Fletcher died at Bethesda, Maryland, on April 23, 1973.

Rear Admiral Raymond Ames Spruance,

commander of Task Force 16 at Midway, attended the U.S. Naval Academy during 1904–06. He did not receive his commission as ensign until 1909 while serving aboard the battleship *Minnesota*. Of all the heroes of Midway, perhaps none deserves the title more than Spruance.

He exhibited rare patience and calm under pressure, refusing to become ruffled in tense situations. Distinguished by a capacity for accepting the advice of his junior officers, yet always trusting ultimately to his own decisions, he more than fulfilled Nimitz's requirement for the right person in the right spot.

Spruance worked at the New York Navy Yard during World War I, then served on a succession of destroyers, battleships, and cruisers, sandwiching in a pair of tours as an instructor at the Naval War College. He commanded the battleship *Mississippi* (1938–39). Promoted to rear admiral in December 1939, he assumed command of the Tenth Naval District (San Juan, Puerto Rico). He was appointed commander of a cruiser division in the Pacific Fleet in November 1941. In that capacity, he provided escort to the carrier *Hornet* during Jimmy Doolittle's Tokyo raid.

Gentle and soft spoken, Spruance lacked the flair of one of his chief supporters, Admiral William F. "Bull" Halsey. But beyond question, Spruance earned at Midway the right to be ranked among the nation's all-time great commanders. A grateful nation will long remember this gentle warrior.

Raymond Ames Spruance died in Pebble Beach, California, on December 13, 1969.

Appendix 2: Principal Aircraft Used in the Battle of Midway

Mitsubishi A6M2 Zero-Sen

No fighter plane has ever symbolized a nation quite like the Zero fighter, excepting possibly the Spitfire. In his book *Famous Fighters of the Second World War*, the noted English aviation writer William Green examines the reality and myth of the Zero.

To the Japanese the Zero-sen was everything that the Spitfire was to the British nation. It symbolized Japan's conduct of the war, for as its fortune fared so fared the Japanese nation. The Zero fighter marked the beginning of a new epoch [age] in naval aviation: it was the first shipboard fighter capable of besting its land-based opponents. It created a myth—the myth of Japanese invincibility in the air, and one to which the Japanese themselves fell victim as a result of the almost total destruction of Allied airpower in the early days of the Pacific war. In its day the Zero was the world's foremost carrier-based fighter, and its appearance over Pearl Harbor came as a complete surprise to the American forces. Its successive appearance over every major battle area in the opening days of the war seemed to indicate that Japan possessed unlimited supplies of this remarkable fighter, and its almost mystical powers of maneuver and ability to traverse vast stretches of water fostered the acceptance of the myth of invincibility in Allied minds.

Jiro Horikoshi, the Zero's designer, liked Mr. Green's description so much that he included the foregoing passage in his own book, *Eagles of Mitsubishi: The Story of the Zero Fighter*.

Grumann F4F Wildcat

At the start of the Pacific war, the unhappy task of fending off the superior Japanese Zero fighter fell largely to the Grumann F4F Wildcat. One navy pilot described it as "a little beer bottle of a plane with a battery of .50-caliber guns in its tiny wings."

Although the Wildcat matched up well with the great Zero in firepower, it was slower, maxing out at 318 miles per hour to the Zero's 331. Nor could the Wildcat climb as fast or turn as sharply as its Japanese opponent. On the plus side, the Wildcat carried more protective armor-plating than the Zero. And it was ruggedly constructed and equipped with self-sealing fuel tanks. In sum, Grumman's stubby little fighter was slower and less maneuverable than the Zero, but harder to shoot down.

In the hands of a veteran pilot, the Wildcat's flaws might have been turned into claws. But in the first grim months after Pearl Harbor, the Americans lacked sadly for experienced combat pilots. Most U.S. Navy pilots were assigned to carrier duty after three hundred hours of flight training without benefit of combat experience. Japanese pilots, on the other hand, joined a carrier only after seven hundred hours in the cockpit. And many who served in the Battle of Midway were veterans of the air war over China that began in 1937.

Although the Wildcat was inferior to the Zero, it had to be used to keep the enemy at a distance until more advanced American fighters could be developed. With skill and the use of tactics, American pilots endured. It might be said that they fought like "wildcats" until Corsairs and Hellcats arrived in the Pacific theater in 1943, ending the Japanese advantage.

Aichi D3A1 Val

The Aichi D3A1, code-named Val by the Allies, claims the distinction of being the last carrier-based aircraft with fixed landing gear. Its more sinister distinction dates back to December 7, 1941, when 125 Vals broke the silence of that Sunday morning during the Japanese attack on Pearl Harbor. The Val, despite its clumsy appearance and modest performance, went on to establish itself as one of the best dive-bombers of its time.

This large single-engined aircraft enjoyed remarkable success during the first year of the

Pacific war. Over the course of its long and far-reaching operational career, the Val succeeded in sinking more Allied warships than any other Japanese bomber. Its more notable victims included the British aircraft carrier *Hermes* and the cruisers *Cornwall* and *Dorsetshire* in April 1942. Thirty-six Val dive-bombers attacked Midway Atoll on the morning of June 4, 1942. Later in the war, the Val closed out its long career—as did many other Japanese airplanes—flying suicide missions.

Douglas TBD-1 Devastator

The Douglas TBD-1 Devastator, the first all-metal, low-wing monoplane with retractable landing gear to enter naval service, was hopelessly obsolete before the Pacific war began. Although the sturdy and reliable Devastator represented advanced design when the aircraft entered service, time and superior designs soon passed it by.

The Battle of Midway quickly proved that the once-proud torpedo bomber could not survive in combat when matched against the fierce fighters of the Japanese. Of the forty-one Devastators committed to battle off the carriers *Enterprise, Yorktown,* and *Hornet*, only five survived. This historic sacrifice to the gods of war ended the combat career of the Devastator, almost before it began. The Devastator, which entered service in November 1937 aboard the carrier *Saratoga*, was retired by the navy after its inadequate performance at Midway.

Nakajima B5N Kate

Like the Aichi Val, the Nakajima B5N, known to the Allies as Kate, was a large, single-engined aircraft. Unlike the Val, the Kate equipped the Japanese navy with what was probably the most advanced aircraft of its kind at the start of the Pacific war. This modern, carrier-based torpedo plane began its long and highly productive combat career at Pearl Harbor. The

144 Kates that took part in the sneak attack against the U.S. Pacific Fleet contributed decisively to the success of Japan's assault.

Capable of delivering both torpedoes and bombs, these sleek machines spelled double trouble for the Allies. The Kates maintained their superiority until late in 1944, when newer, more effective Allied aircraft began to take their measure. When the Imperial Navy finally retired them from front-line duty, the Kates left behind a record of accomplishment not easily forgotten. Not the least among their successes—beginning at Midway—were their attacks on the American carriers *Yorktown, Lexington*, and *Hornet*, resulting in the sinking of all three vessels.

Douglas SBD Dauntless

No greater dive-bomber than the Douglas SBD Dauntless lifted off the wave-tossed deck of any aircraft carrier during the Second World War. A tough, compact, single-engined monoplane, it served both navy and marine pilots and crews with distinction until the end of 1944, when it was reassigned to a secondary role. But many Dauntlesses survived the war and remained in service for some years afterward.

The Dauntless first distinguished itself during the Battle of the Coral Sea, when SBDs off the American carriers *Yorktown* and *Lexington* sank the Japanese carrier *Shoho* on May 7, 1942. Beyond question, however, it was during the Battle of Midway that the Dauntless staked its claim to immortality.

In "six minutes that changed the world," SBDs off *Yorktown* and *Enterprise* screamed down from heights of twenty thousand feet to bomb and sink the Japanese carriers *Soryu, Kaga*, and *Akagi* on June 4, 1942. Later that day, more Dauntlesses delivered mortal blows to the carrier *Hiryu*. Still more Dauntlesses completed "the miracle at Midway" by sinking the Japanese heavy cruiser *Mikuma* on June 6.

Index

Because of the frequency of mentions, ships are not named, except carriers, nor planes unless discussed or described.

Picture Credits

Cover photo: National Archives

Archive Photos, 88 (bottom)

Library of Congress, 12 (top), 21, 30, 50 (both), 52, 55, 88 (top), 92

National Archives, 11, 12 (bottom), 13, 15 (all), 16, 18 (both), 20, 23 (both), 26, 27, 29 (both), 33, 34, 35, 40, 41, 42, 43, 44, 47 (both), 49, 54, 60 (both), 61, 62, 64, 65, 66 (both), 68, 69, 71, 73, 74, 76 (both), 77, 79, 80, 84, 87, 90

Smithsonian Institution, 81, 94

UPI/Bettmann, 31, 56, 57, 67, 86, 91

About the Author

Earle Rice Jr. attended San Jose City College and Foothill College on the San Francisco peninsula, after serving nine years with the U.S. Marine Corps.

He has authored ten books for young adults, including fast-action fiction and adaptations of *Dracula* and *All Quiet on the Western Front*. Mr. Rice has written several books for Lucent, including *The Cuban Revolution* and *The Battle of Britain*. He has also written articles and short stories, and he worked for several years as a technical writer.

Mr. Rice is a former senior design engineer in the aerospace industry who now devotes full time to his writing. He lives in Julian, California, with his wife, daughter, granddaughter, four cats, and a dog.